Covenant to Care

Formerly, Creative Love

Louis H. Evans, Jr.

This book is intended for personal reading and group study. A leader's guide with helps and hints for teachers and visual aids (Victor Multiuse Transparency Masters) is available from your local bookstore or from the publisher.

VICTOR BOOKS

a division of SP Publications, Inc.

WHEATON. ILLINOIS 60187

Offices also in Fullerton, California • Whitby, Ontario, Canada • Amersham-on-the-Hill, Bucks, England

Unless otherwise identified, Scripture quotations are from the *Revised Standard Version of the Bible,* ©1946, 1952, 1971 and 1973. Scripture quotations identified PH are from *The New Testament in Modern English* by J. B. Phillips, ©1958, 1959, 1960 by The MacMillan Company. Used by permission. Scriptures identified KJV are from the King James Version.

Covenant to Care was originally titled *Creative Love,* published by Spire Books. The author revised and updated it for republication.

Recommended Dewey Decimal Classification: 248.4
  Suggested Subject Headings: CHRISTIAN LIFE; BEHAVIOR;
    SPIRITUAL LIFE

Library of Congress Catalog Card Number: 81-86104
ISBN: 0-88207-355-9

VICTOR BOOKS
A division of SP Publications, Inc.
P.O. Box 1825 • Wheaton, IL 60187

Contents

To Colleen, my primary covenant partner,
whose firm commitment has been an untiring resource,
and my covenant brothers and sisters,
who have taught me so much of covenant dynamics.

A Personal Pilgrimage

(Introduction)

Covenant relationships of openness and shared need have not come naturally to me. To realize my strengths and weaknesses and admit them to covenant brothers and sisters is something I've had to learn on a personal pilgrimage. Like old Abram, I had to leave one country—the land of self-sufficiency and strong individualism—and go to another land— a place of interdependence and honest love; a place to share dreams and visions. I would like to tell you how my pilgrimage began.

I suppose you could have called me Mr. Independent. The first air I breathed was fragrant with the pungent odor of vitality, creative energy, and success. Dad was alive with the kingdom of God, stirring each church he pastored with dynamic personal warmth, masterful preaching, and strong pastoral care. Grandfather (we never dared call him *Granddad*) was a world-renowned Bible scholar and lecturer, holding crowds on the edges of their seats with his unforgettable imagery and rhetoric. His forty books, some of which are still used in Bible schools and colleges today, illustrated his master craftsmanship and relentless discipline. Mother was a combination of feminine warmth and good old German pietism, plus a healthy dose of love for hard work and an ecstatic love for God's nature. I can still remember seeing the sweat rolling from her face as she worked the laundry plunger by hand when the washing machine broke down, saying with excitement, "Work is good, Louis, Junior— work is good!" I remember hearing her cry out with joy as she turned her desert-trained eyes toward a vivid sunset and re- called racing across the wet Arizona sage on her favorite mare after a rain.

A boy could not have wanted a better home—love, joy, and adventure, all mixed together. Out of those materials I was to build my future.

I started building my edifice, taking the blocks around me and putting them into a tower of my own design. Unknowingly, I took the stone of excessive amibition and put that with the blocks of unrealistic scheduling, perfectionism, and self- sufficiency—all of them set in the mortar of an inability to com- municate my inward feelings. Little did I know my tower was to become a prison—grand in some sense of personal success but holding me aloof from other people.

The first indications of a problem, which I refused to recog- nize, were periods of quietness and, at times, sullenness. They would go on for days. The household was so busy that it was difficult for others to pick up the clues; I certainly didn't. Then, as president of both the student body at Hollywood High School and the College Department of the First Presbyterian Church of Hollywood, I completely failed to hear what people were saying and *feeling* when they spoke about a young man they respected and liked but couldn't get to know. I thought such loneliness was a part of leadership.

Later, in my first parish, rampant hay fever sent me into paroxysms of sneezing so that one day while I was making a pastoral visit, much to my chagrin, a sophisticated matron told me to go home. Then there were back problems with periods of spasms that could be explained by a bad disk (too much broad jumping, football, and masonry, we all thought), chronic kidney or bladder infections, and migraine headaches. That's all! A walking casebook of psychosomatic symptoms—that's what I was but so defensive about it that each symptom had to carry a purely physical explanation. From time to time Dr. Lee Travis, a psychologist and one of the world's great therapists, then a new Christian, would put his long arm around my shoulder and look at me with warm concern and ask, "Louis, how *are* you?" I would always blurt out, "Oh, fine, Lee, great!" even though one of the "Four Horsemen" of my symptoms was galloping across my aching body.

Although in the midst of happy people and doing "successful" things, I was a loner! You could have called me a product of the Standard American Package—the rugged individualism of the frontier days, the self-sufficiency of my Plains-farmer forerunners who had to do everything for themselves, the lead-from-strength emphasis of the successful American executive, and the Jesus-and-I-can-do-it-together theology. When a problem came up, I took it all to Jesus, and we did pretty well. But I cut others out of my life. When my wife Colleen would say, "Honey, there are times I feel you just don't need me," I could see the pain in her lovely face because she needed to be needed, but I found it difficult to understand. Couldn't she see how much I needed her, how I ached for help at times? Somehow I had never communicated that to her. I had learned my standard American lesson very well: "Don't wear your heart on your sleeve; folks have enough problems of their own; don't bother them with yours; keep it to yourself."

True, a beautiful thing had happened to me when I met Christ in a rather body-slamming experience. He gave me a good look at my arrogance and conceit, which shattered my composure. But, bless Him, when I turned my life over to Him to use as He saw fit, He responded by giving me a sense of cleansing I shall never forget or lose and a call to the ministry that was a tremendous motivation! That experience was the greatest thing that ever happened to me, but it intensified the problem. Now I had a consuming goal on which to focus all those excessive ambitions and unrealistic schedules!

The Change

Little did I know it, but the stimuli for change began to collect in life. The first was Colleen, whom most everyone calls "Coke." One night during our early dating experience, we walked up the bridle trail that leads to the planetarium in the Hollywood hills. In chivalrous fashion, I put down my letterman sweater, and we both sat on it. Something had begun to develop between Coke and me since our spiritual awakenings six months earlier. With the city of Los Angeles spread before us and its myriad twinkling lights, I was terribly conscious of our aloneness and the beauty of this woman. Then she said, "Louie, tell me about yourself." A sense of excitement and exhilaration shot through me. It was a combination of feelings, I suppose, being asked that question by a young movie star about whom all the country was talking; my own growing feeling of closeness to her (I thought I would explode if I touched her!); but more than anything else, the fact that she wanted to know me. In the fast-paced world of success, who stopped long enough to ask such a question?

I found it difficult to begin, so I poked with a twig in the sand for a moment. Her arms were crossed on her knees, and she was leaning forward slightly, looking straight at me, patiently, expectantly. How could I refuse? Haltingly, I began to tell her about myself. For the life of me, I can't remember what I said, but I was talking! I was telling someone about myself, my hopes, and my dreams for the ministry. I don't think I said much about the pain of my shyness and my feelings of insufficiency. I think she sensed the shyness, but the insufficiency was well hidden.

Starting at that moment, Coke was to be my teacher more than anyone else in relational matters. Her love and honesty made that easy.

For her own reasons and for my own, we had a limit to our communication in spite of the good start. The part that was difficult for both of us was sharing our anger and our pain not only with one another but with others. Everywhere around us were symbols of success. She was the subject of a cover article in *Life;* I was freshman-class president at Occidental College and still president of the College Department at the church. Dad had the largest church in the denomination. And then there was Hollywood itself. Who talks about failure or pain in a setting like that? Besides, I had not learned to express my anger or frustration in a healthy manner, and Coke was reluctant to stir the waters. So how were we to express our negative feelings to one another? It was difficult. They were stored up inside. The process of emptying the storage closet began in our first parish in Bel Air, California, with our *mirror* encounter (to be explained later). That began the process of honest sharing for us. We spent many beautiful, many painful hours together learning this new art. Two things held us in our pursuit of this communication process: our deep love and commitment to each other and our confidence that God would give us whatever resources we needed.

After we went to the La Jolla church, a new facet was ground. The encounter-group method was running at high tide in that seacoast town with Carl Rogers and the Western Behavioral Science Institute. I attended one of their week-long seminars, and by Wednesday they had discovered that I was a gold mine for encounter! Can you imagine a preacher-type, unable to share pain, self-contained, in such a group? I remember so vividly at one point a man from Colorado stood in front of me with his hands outstretched, his eyes brimming, and his face contorted with emotion. In a choking voice he said, "Louie, can you touch me?"

I was embarrassed, not knowing what to do, and finally took hold of his hands. For what seemed like an eternity, we just looked at each other, until someone in the group asked, "Do you know what he's trying to say to you?"

Again, silence reigned.

Then a woman explained: "He's trying to tell you what a lot of us feel—that we have no place in your life."

The truth hurt: my self-sufficiency was blocking others out, and their pain was intense. They felt they had something to give me, but I would not allow them to give it. It all added up to a form of rejection from someone they cared about. They were attempting to show me their love, but my castle gate was closed and the drawbridge was up! No way could they get in!

Believe me, they tagged me for a couple of other things that week! When it was all over, I felt a kind of gratitude for their honesty and yet a rejection. I had made some of them angry. One fellow, an eager executive type who I felt was constantly taking me on for sheer competition, blurted out in real hostility, "Don't you ever be a group leader, Mr. Insensitive!" For a long time I wasn't; his remark had cut deeply.

Like a kitchen surgeon, the group had gotten out some of my problems and had left them on the table. In the succeeding days I longed to get those parts back into my bone and muscle, but the group wasn't there to help. They had gone to their homes, and I would never see them again.

In my pain, I went to my close friend and associate Gordon Hess and poured out my frustration. "Gordie, there's got to be some way of achieving the honesty these folks demonstrated— but in a continuing relationship that can help me put myself together again. And I missed the freedom to talk about Christ and His part in the whole process. Somehow I felt He wants to be an active member of such a group."

Gordie concurred, and under his leadership *spiritual-growth* groups were formed in the La Jolla Presbyterian Church. To the honesty and openness of our encounter groups were added some of the things we had seen demonstrated in Faith at Work groups—the warm affirmation plus the freedom to speak of Christ and to share His redeeming and liberating power with one another.

At one point the Rev. Dick Spencer, with whom I was associated, arranged for the Faith at Work folks to come in and "do a weekend" with the interested members from La Jolla Presbyterian plus those from other churches. That weekend 325 people were blessed with a type of small-group sharing that took the restraints off the process of talking about Christ and telling others of the experiences we were having with Him. Prior to this, religion was "a personal thing," which meant that most people were ill at ease with any personalized expression or witness. Once we began sharing openly what Christ was doing, scores leaped ahead in their spiritual growth and emotional maturation.

From time to time, several of us attended workshops conducted by Keith Miller, Bruce Larson, Lloyd Ogilvie, Ralph Osborne, Ben Johnson, Heidi Frost, Stan Jones, and a number of others. They were our teachers, and how grateful I am to them for showing us the nature of Christian relationships.

It was all quite new to me, and yet it was not new to the faith. I was simply learning in a contemporary setting what Christians and Jews had known for thousands of years.

I know there are all types of groups and "groupies" today, but I am especially interested in what I call the *covenant* groups. They may be called by others *koinonia* groups, *agape* groups, *spiritual growth* groups, *support* groups, or other titles. Their common characteristics are the covenant and committed relationships with an honest, Christian community.

The archetype of the biblical covenant group would be like the one suggested to Moses by his father-in-law Jethro, after he saw Moses bowing under the heavy burden of counseling as he tried to govern and teach the Hebrew children following years of Egyptian bondage. The task was about to do him in.

Jethro came down to visit Moses after the first skirmish with the Amalekites. Moses had sent his wife Zipporah, and the two boys, Gershom and Eliezer, to his father-in-law for safekeeping during the battle. Jethro listened intently as Moses shared all that God had done in delivering the Hebrew children from the Egyptians.

I can picture it now: The next day Jethro gets up at a decent hour but notices that Moses already has been long at his work; there he sits on the floor of the desert with a crowd of people gathered about him, pressing and pushing as though trying to get his attention. That goes on all day. Finally, as the sun sets, Jethro sees Moses raise his hands in a kind of blessing to dismiss the people. As the crowd disperses, Moses trudges his weary way up the little incline to the place where his tent overlooks the whole camp of the Israelites. Jethro notices that Moses' shoulders sag with fatigue; his hair has a wild, electric look from the wind and sand that has dried it out; his eyes are sunk in dark sockets, the kind we often see in our presidents after years of unrelenting pressures. As Moses sits on a rock near his tent and lowers his chiseled features into gnarled shepherd hands, Zipporah comes from the tent and puts her arms about him momentarily. To show concern for her man, she shrouds her face. She gives him a refreshing drink, and Moses thanks her tenderly with a voice hoarse with fatigue.

Jethro asks, "What is this that you are doing for the people? Why do you sit alone, and all the people stand about you from morning till evening?"

And Moses says to his father-in-law, "Because the people come to me to inquire of God; when they have a dispute, they come to me, and I decide between a man and his neighbor, and I make them know the statutes of God and His decisions" (Exodus 18:14-16).

Then Jethro says, "What you are doing is not good. You and the people will wear yourselves out, for this thing is too heavy for you; you are not able to perform it alone. Listen now to my voice; I will give you counsel, and God be with you! You shall represent the people before God, and bring their cases to God; and you shall teach them the statutes and the decisions, and make them know the way in which they must walk and what they must do. Moreover choose able men from all the people, such as fear God, men who are trustworthy and who hate a bribe, and place such men over the people as rulers of thousands, of hundreds, of fifties, and of tens. And let them judge the people at all times; every great matter they shall bring to you, but any small matter they shall decide themselves; so it will be easier for you, and they will bear the burden with you. If you do this, and God so commands you, then you shall be able to endure, and all this people also will go to their place in peace" (Exodus 18:17-23).

There it was—the foundation of the small group movement. Out of sheer necessity, the congregation of hundreds of thousands was broken down into small clusters of concern. The group of ten became known in the Jewish culture as the *minyan* and was the core or cellular structure that saw the Jewish people through centuries of persecution and trial. Why have they remained so strong? There are many explanations, I am sure, but I am convinced that one of the great reasons for their fortitude and strength is the *minyan.* Here men could come and share their burdens, celebrate the birth of their children, receive comfort on the death of their parents, and pray the yearly *kaddishim,* the prayers for the dead. Here was a counseling group for business or personal difficulties; this was the worshiping group. So much of life took place in the *minyan,* the covenant group if Israel.

Christ and His disciples had this same type of group. Jesus said, "You are My friends" (John 15:14), probably using the Hebrew word *chaber* which means "one bound to me, my companion." John's chronology indicates that Christ had been taken off the cross quickly so that He would not be there during the feast of the Passover. If the Passover was celebrated the night of His death, then what was the occasion the night before when Jesus ate the last meal with His disciples? It was probably a *chaburah* in which close friends (*chaberim*) got together to prepare for the feasts of the Jews. Part of such a meal was eating the bread of covenant and drinking the cup of joy as they reaffirmed their loyalty to one another and to their leader or cause. It was at this time at the table that Christ said, "Drink of it, all of you; for this is My blood of the covenant, which is poured out for many for the forgiveness of sins" (Matthew 26:27-28). It was indeed a covenant group—a *minyan* that had found its ultimate expression.

In this group Jesus had been available to the disciples in a way He was not available to the throngs. He had shared His inmost feelings with them, His dreams of the Kingdom, His fatigue, His anger, His heartache. These were His men, His *chaberim*—his covenant brothers, if you will.

The Apostle Paul also had his traveling group. Its constituency changed from time to time, but they were always there, ministering to one another, constantly praying for one another—brothers and sisters in a covenant relationship that was characterized by healing, honesty, untiring love, dedicated laboring, and fellowship in learning and suffering. Paul had covenanted to these people in the good Jewish tradition of the *minyan*. He was totally available!

So, small groups are nothing new.

I know that some of the contemporary groups leave a lot to be desired. In fact, we have to resist much of what goes on in some groups as detrimental to long-range human relationships. But, in spite of the distortions—and they are gross at times—groups continue to be one of God's unique instruments in spiritual awakening. They always have been present at times of revival, and I believe they always will be.

What follows are some of my ideas and insights, gleaned in these last twelve years of my personal walk and ministry. They are certainly not complete, nor are they all necessarily one hundred percent correct. I am still in the process of discovery and share these with you in an effort to be part of what God is doing in the life of the church, His beloved body, today.

What follows are not laws; they are principles, dynamics, guidelines—flexible and with applications differing in each group.

And groups are not for everybody, all of the time. Some find them quite offensive, for they have been trained to live privately and either are not ready to share or find their personalities not in tune. No one should feel guilty or be made to feel guilty for not participating. God has His times and seasons for each of us. It was some time before I felt comfortable enough to join the group experience. What helped me most was those folks who loved me and put a warm example in front of me that I could not resist forever. They did not pressure or push but simply witnessed. I saw such honesty and growth coming into their lives that I wanted some of the same.

For those interested in covenant groups, I put forth these thoughts in hopes that others may go far beyond my early and stumbling efforts.

Welcome to the covenants! *Shalom chaberim.*

1 What Are "Covenant Groups"?

My need for a continued relationship with other people led me to my first covenant group. The group began because a few couples agreed to meet once a week to try to understand: (1) more about what God was saying in the Bible as it related to us, and (2) more about ourselves. Initially, we simply agreed to be honest with each other, later calling it the *covenant of honesty*. Over a period of years other covenants emerged until now there are eight, all helping us understand what Jesus meant by His own covenant style. Possibly there could be more, but this just happens to be where the ball stopped rolling at the time of this writing. The covenants are those of

Affirmation
Availability
Prayer
Openness
Honesty
Sensitivity
Confidentiality
Accountability.

In presenting these covenants I would like to give examples from the covenant style of the Master whom most of the world

17

accepts as a great teacher but who is to me much more. In His death and resurrection, He is indeed Saviour, again and again breaking those bonds that hold us prisoner, and setting us free to that life which He has designed in His love for each of us. But He not only liberates, He takes us through the processes of healing and therapy until we are able to take our places in the productive stream of society.

Since participating in that first group, I have learned that committing a regular portion of our time to another person becomes one of the most meaningful things we can do. It says to that person, "You are important to me." On the contrary, when we won't give another person the time of day, we are saying, "You don't matter that much to me." Christ uniquely gives the sort of love that is willing to make the time commitment. I don't mean that a person cannot have a loving, committed relationship unless he has the love of Christ within him, but the chances aren't that great. Nor is it necessary to be in a covenant group in order to make its characteristics part of one's life.

Yet, each of us participates in some kind of covenant group, whether we realize it or not: our families, our communities, our schools, or our churches. Through such groups, we experience and express the power of love; as love beings, we cannot grow without the love of others. We either respond to the love and grow, or we hold tightly to ourselves, failing to move out to others, and consequently atrophy. These covenant groups are the laboratories where we try out life and where real people are identified and given resources.

The family in which each of us grew up was the first covenant group to which we belonged. Depending on the quality of that covenant group, we can either relate well in covenant or find relating difficult. If covenant was not experienced there, of course, that is a significant disadvantage. But life does not stop at that point. Christ in His healing power can introduce us to the covenants of His redemptive community; old hungers can be met and old wounds healed. We can make up for the lean years so satisfyingly that we almost forget the pain and starvation of the former years. We are not bound to our pasts: we are not closed systems limited to the computer inputs of the past. We are open systems, open to the love of God that can transform our lives from what they tragically were to the glorious way He wants them to be.

A covenant relationship implies that whatever we have is available to our covenant brothers and sisters, and this is a promise we can make only to a limited number of people. This may disturb us if we feel that we must be equally available to all we meet, but if we are that sort, we are probably torn by our excessive response to the needs of humanity around us. I have suffered from that available-to-all attempt, burning up deep reserves in surprisingly short periods of time, only to fall into periods of depression, psychosomatic illnesses, and lagging motivation. Our Lord chose the Twelve "to be with Him" (Mark 3:14) evidently in a manner different from His relation to the masses. They had a claim on His time as the crowds did not. There were occasions when He left the crying multitudes on the beach and sought out times with His disciples.

This does not mean that we treat the world outside covenant relationships with an attitude of exclusion. Rather, when we are called to minister to the world, we can give all the more, because we have received so fully from the covenant relationships.

"But what will happen to the rest of the world?" you ask.

If all of us enter into the covenant relationships proper for us, then all will have the quality of relationships needed to cope with life. Each of us is only one voice in the choir of humanity; we cannot sing anyone else's part or make up for his failures. If we will live qualitatively with those with whom we are in covenant, the results will multiply like leaven in a lump of dough. Ferment is God's pattern of reproduction. We cannot suckle the whole world; we are not called to be messiahs, but simply servants of a few.

Principles of Covenant Groups

Covenant groups are an expression of our life in Christ. These groups cannot reach their potential unless Christ is an active member. Our life and strength flow from Him; therefore, we can take joy in His presence and express what He is accomplishing in our group.

His Word is our guide and therefore, it should be used as the group feels the need. It is out of His Word that we identify the following covenant dynamics:

1. *The covenant of affirmation (unconditional love, agape love)*: There is nothing you have done or will do that will make me stop loving you. I may not agree with your actions, but I will love you as a person and do all I can to hold you up in God's affirming love.

2. *The covenant of availability*: Anything I have—time, energy, insight, possessions—is at your disposal if you need it, to the limit of my resources. I give these to you in a priority of covenant over other noncovenant demands. As part of this availability, I pledge my time on a regular basis, whether in prayer or in an agreed-on meeting time.

3. *The covenant of prayer*: I covenant to pray for you in some regular fashion, believing that our caring Father wishes His children to pray for one another and ask Him for the blessings they need.

4. *The covenant of openness*: I promise to strive to become a more open person, disclosing my feelings, my struggles, my joys, and my hurts to you as well as I am able. The degree to which I do so implies that I cannot make it without you, that I trust you with my problems and my dreams, and that I need you. This is to affirm your worth to me as a person. In other words, I need you!

5. *The covenant of honesty*: I will try to mirror back to you what I am hearing you say and feel. If this means risking pain for either of us, I will trust our relationship enough to take that risk, realizing it is in "speaking the truth in love"

that we grow up in every way into Christ who is the head (Ephesians 4:15). I will try to express this honesty in a sensitive and controlled manner and to meter it, according to what I perceive the circumstances to be.

6. *The covenant of sensitivity:* Even as I desire to be known and understood by you, I covenant to be sensitive to you and to your needs to the best of my ability. I will try to hear you, see you, and feel where you are and to draw you out of the pit of discouragement or withdrawal.

7. *The covenant of confidentiality:* I will promise to keep whatever is shared within the confines of the group in order to provide the atmosphere of openness.

8. *The covenant of accountability:* I consider that the gifts God has given me for the common good should be liberated for your benefit. If I should discover areas of my life that are under bondage, hung up, or truncated by my own misdoings or by the scars inflicted by others, I will seek Christ's liberating power through His Holy Spirit and through my covenant partners so that I might give to you more of myself. I am accountable to you to become what God has designed me to be in His loving creation.

The following chapters explain some of my thoughts and feelings about these covenant principles and some of my experiences with my covenant brothers and sisters.

2 The Biblical Basis of Covenant

"Just what do you mean by *covenant*?" That question has been asked so many times that I had better stop here and make an attempt at a definition. A covenant is a solemn promise made by one or more persons who do not intend to break that promise. It is a promise that perseveres in spite of difficulties or inconveniences, in which the covenantor says, "Because I love you I will not desert the covenant."

The best way I can explain what I mean by *covenant* is to go to the Scriptures and let them portray the characteristics of a covenant relationship. God is a covenant-making God. From His covenant-making we get some clues as to what He expects of us because we are creatures of His image.

A number of Old Testament passages and one New Testament passage form the basis of a brief study. Certainly this is not extensive nor complete. In fact, it is embarrassingly simple. I am confident, however, that you can do your own study and make additions and improvements in this exciting subject.

The Old Testament passages we will peruse are Genesis 9, the story of Noah; Genesis 15, the account of God making a covenant with Abram; Jeremiah 31, sometimes called the passage on the New Covenant; Ezekiel 37; and Hosea 2-6.

God Takes the Initiative

In each of these Old Testament passages, God takes the initiative in making a covenant. In Genesis 9, when the massive waters retreated from the face of the earth, God made a covenant with Noah, symbolized in the rainbow, that never again would the earth be destroyed by water. God in His careful love took the initiative to ease the anxiety and fear of coming generations (Genesis 9).

When God told Abram to look at the stars and try to number them, He took the initiative to make a covenant promising sons in vast numbers, a land for them to dwell in, and a blessing to all families of the earth through Abram's descendants (Genesis 15:1-6).

Whenever the other passages speak of the establishment of covenant, God always takes the initiative. This is in spite of the waywardness and rejection of the people, their faithlessness and blatant disregard. For God to take the initiative is simply God being faithful to His own character. He cannot deny Himself (2 Timothy 2:13) though all others prove faithless.

God by His very nature is a covenant-making God.

How About Us?

"Then God said, 'Let Us make man in Our image, after Our likeness. . . .' So God created man in His own image, in the image of God He created him" (Genesis 1:26-27). Being creatures in the image of God, we too are creatures of covenant, hungering to receive covenant and hungering to make covenants. To make covenants is inherent to our natures. Until we receive and give such unconditional promises, we never realize our full identity as created in the image of God. We too must take the initiative in establishing covenants if we are going to be fully human.

Our great temptation is to wait for somebody else to make the first move. Perhaps we feel it would be risking rejection or be presumptuous to take such a lead. Yet, the magnificent things of life take place when someone noble enough, strong enough, with some degree of fearlessness breaks the silence with quiet, strong words of promise that will not be blown away before the winds of circumstance, nor melted by the passions of anger, nor shattered by the sickening blows of failure.

God took the initiative. Let us do likewise—in the image of God.

Covenant Is Sometimes Unilateral

We usually think of a covenant as being shared by two or more people. But sometimes covenant is unilateral, one person making the covenant in the absence or the ignorance of the other.

After God had promised the covenant, Abram cried out, "O Lord God, how am I to know that I shall possess it [the covenant]?" (Genesis 15:8) God answered by giving instructions for him to cut in two pieces a heifer, a she-goat, and a ram and lay the pieces opposite each other with a turtle dove and pigeon. Evidently this arrangement was in preparation for some ceremony of covenant-making. After following the instructions, Abram waited patiently throughout the long hot day for the ceremony. Buzzards came to peck away at the carcasses, but Abram drove them away. Finally, the sun set; dusk's quiet stillness touched his eyes with the heaviness of sleep.

And while he slept, a smoking fire pot and a firebrand passed between the pieces laid out, evidently inaugurating the covenant God had promised. However, Abram was not conscious of it.

For years this story bothered me. If God was making the covenant with Abram, why was the old shepherd asleep when the ceremony establishing the covenant was performed? Could it be that God was saying the covenant did not depend upon the consciousness of the other party nor the bilateral nature of the agreement, but upon His action alone? This appears to be the most probable explanation. Evidently God acted unilaterally. He did not wait for recriprocation.

A number of times I have seen persons making unilateral covenants with others who were not conscious of the covenant or even rejected it. If they were conscious of the promise, they certainly did not reciprocate.

I watched one woman who often came to our home to seek counsel from my father and receive encouragement and strength to go on with a tough marriage. For seventeen years she endured the drunken abuse of herself and the two girls; verbal onslaughts, physical beatings, insensitive advances. Then one day her husband responded to the invitation of Christ at a Billy Graham Crusade. After the conversion he still had some rough traits, but his life was transformed. Many times he witnessed to the fact that her love and covenant which would not give up was God's key tool in bringing him to this experience of Christ that changed their marriage.

She had persevered in a unilateral covenant. Happily, the covenant is now returned by her partner; he has reciprocated joyously and gratefully. It all began with her unilateral promise that would not quit.

Keep on Covenanting
Once may not be enough.

The covenant God made with Abram was magnanimous, generous, and filled with hope. Yet it was not without its demands and challenges that required effort and danger on the part of the recipients of the covenant. God told them to go in and take the land. However, in coming into possession of the land God had promised, the people of Israel had to risk their safety in going across a Jordan River swollen with seasonal rains, and take by force a land of fortified cities whose inhabitants were as giants. A formidable task! The prospect frightened them; it paralyzed them with fear. Not being sure God could bring off what He had commanded them to do, they dug in their heels of disobedience and stayed where they were—in the desert of Nowhere. Refusing to believe God and thus obey Him, they fearfully turned their backs on his delivering power which they had experienced coming out of Egypt. They played it safe.

This angered God. He called it rebellion. To Him it was a

breaking of the covenant He had made with them through Abram, the covenant He repeated to Isaac, Jacob, and Joseph. In His wrath He swore that their generation would not enter into His rest; they would die in the wilderness.

Nevertheless, centuries later, God renewed His covenant with the future generations of Israel. In Jeremiah 31, we see God making a New Covenant with the house of Judah and the house of Israel. Though they had refused Him, shaken their fists of disobedience in His face, He persevered in the covenant-making process and made a New Covenant described by Jeremiah:

Behold, the days are coming, says the Lord, when I will make a New Covenant with the house of Israel and the house of Judah, not like the covenant which I made with their fathers when I took them by the hand to bring them out of the land of Egypt, My covenant which they broke, though I was their husband, says the Lord. But this is the covenant which I will make with the house of Israel after those days, says the Lord: I will put My law within them, and I will write it upon their hearts; and I will be their God, and they shall be My people. And no longer shall each man teach his neighbor each his brother, saying, "Know the Lord," for they shall all know Me, from the least of them to the greatest, says the Lord; for I will forgive their iniquity, and I will remember their sins no more (Jeremiah 31:31-34).

God persevered in covenant-making in spite of the failure of the people. There are times we too must persevere in a covenant when disappointment, failure, and anger will tempt us to throw in the towel and call an end to the covenant. The tough love of God will not let this happen; it will stay on top with a patience born of the Holy Spirit and cry out, "There is nothing you can do, there is nothing you can say that will ever make me stop loving you or call an end to our covenant!"

That is persevering love. God was the first to model it; we are to follow in His example.

Three Marks of the New Covenant

Notice three marks of the New Covenant as outlined by Jeremiah.

1. *It will be an internalized covenant.* "I will put My law *within* them, and I will write it upon their hearts" (v. 33).

In the field of psychotherapy there is a process called *cathecting.* To cathect is to get an identity or feeling up into one's psyche so that it becomes a part of the person, a part of the core of personality. Sometimes the process of cathecting is pathological as when a person cathects an identity not his or her own. Then life is lived in a counterfeit manner. Therapy attempts to purge this identity so that the real self may be cathected.

On the other hand, cathecting can be a healthy process. When children experience the deep love every human desires from parents, or feels that the important others in life consider them worthy of love simply because they are themselves, these children cathect these experiences and feelings and build a basis for security. This becomes the foundation of fearlessness, a source of willingness to venture out into life and a resource to risk being creative.

In the New Covenant, God fulfills His promise in that the Holy Spirit convinces us that we are the loved children of God so that our inner being cries out, "Abba, Father!" Such an outcry is the exultation of confidence and security of being loved. When we cathect that love of God, we are able to venture out into the difficult tasks of the kingdom, storming the gates of hell that will not be able to withstand the onslaught of love.

The kingdom tasks are difficult and demand far more than we are able to give as humans. However, being assured of God's love and the constancy of His provision, we are able to cross our Jordans' swirling waters and take the land on the other side. Our foes are just as formidable today as those of the Israelites; we too will cower in disbelief and fear if we do not have this inner witness of the Holy Spirit. This is the reason we can never diminish our emphasis either on the evangelical experience of knowing God as a loving and forgiving Father who gives us new life in the birth of the Spirit, or on the ministries of reconciliation in a world torn by bigotry, oppression, and alienation. If either of these emphases is lost in the Christian life, we deny the design of God and fall short of the kingdom of God. With this inner witness of the Spirit, we can march through hell and back and never even smell of smoke. The confidence will be so strong that we will not even remember the horrors or the difficulties we went through. They will not be able to affect our future behavior; the past will have no dominion or limiting influence over us. The triumphant cry of Martin Luther King, Jr. was a modern evidence of this confidence: "Free at last, free at last, thank God Almighty, I'm free at last!" The whole world is standing on tiptoe, longing to see the children of God gain this liberty! (Romans 8:19)

2. *The New Covenant is an intimate covenant,* one of close personal relationship with God.

> I will be their God, and they shall be My people. And no longer shall each man teach his neighbor and each his brother, saying, "Know the Lord," for they shall all know Me, from the least of them to the greatest" (Jeremiah 31:33-34).

Ezekiel repeats the same promise: "They shall not defile themselves any more with their idols and their detestable things. . . . I will save them from all the backslidings in which they have sinned, and will cleanse them; and they shall be My people, and I will be their God" (Ezekiel 37:23).

"My dwelling place shall be with them; and I will be their God, and they shall be My people" (Ezekiel 37:27).

Hosea takes up the same theme: "I will betroth you to Me in faithfulness; and you shall know the Lord" (Hosea 2:20).

The words used for *know* in these passages are interesting, for they give a clue as to the kind of knowing there will be. It is an intimate knowing. Hosea likens it to that of a man and wife in the intimacies of marriage's most personal moments. Jeremiah speaks of knowing as an insightful, "aha" discovery of another's thoughts and feelings. There is nothing distant or guarded. The knowing is that of transparency and openness to the other. Nothing is hidden from the beloved. That is the sort of intimacy to which God calls us. The closest, most personal intimacy imaginable.

This intimacy is that of a child joyfully shouting, "Daddy!" It speaks of immeasurable confidence, the joy of being in another's presence, the memory of the happy past and the dreams of the anticipated future. It is dreaming together about tomorrow, sharing life's most intimate secrets, walking out of the valley of fear or difficulty hand in hand into the warmth of God's rich sunlight. The intimacy is that which a child knows as he or she rests on Father's sturdy shoulder, pressing close in speechless communication, hearing his heart beat, strong and firm, and hearing the words, "You are my child, and I am your daddy. I love you; I love you."

The intimacy of covenant relationship is the seeing of a need the world might never see under a mask of self-sufficiency and strength. Intimacy is the acquisition of personal data, those telltale bits of information or intuition gathered over the years, that are pieces of a mosaic making clear the answer in decision-making counseling. Intimacy is the intuition that accurately calculates the resources of the other in times of stress and rushes reinforcements to the scene. Intimacy is sharing the limited resources of time, energy, finances, and possessions in common submission and ministry. It is the adjusting of one's schedule to that of the covenant partner; the cooperation in mundane details that bonds covenant partners in a strong fellowship. It is the warm and at times aching desire to be with another, and the shout of delight, the embrace of joy when seeing the covenant brother or sister.

Thank God for the intimacies of covenant!

3. *God's New Covenant is one of forgiveness and forgetting.*
God the forgiver is the One who was injured. The forgiver is the
one who is disappointed at the failure of the other, or wounded
by the words or actions of the forgiven. The motive of forgiveness is simple—to be in full relationship as quickly as possible,
to remove the barriers to relationship that the tide of love may
ebb and flow once again.

Forgiveness is trudging down the road with tear-shrouded
eyes in a determination to find the one who is separated and
throw arms of love about him or her. Forgiveness leaps over
the hurdles of pride and walks around the piles of relational
debris to lift the partner out of the ashes of remorse and alienation.

God's forgetting goes hand in hand with His forgiving. His
forgiving is so complete that He sets aside forever the past and
concentrates on the future.

That is exactly what He wants us to do, both in forgiving
others as well as ourselves. Too often we remember the past.
Such memory binds us; it controls our reactions. If we hold the
memory of another's misdeeds toward us or if we nurture the
memories of our own misdoings, we are not free to make decisions without constantly referring back to the memories. Life
becomes a huge reaction, something like trying to drive down a
highway looking at the rearview mirror. The only clues we have
are in the past. We are much too slow to see or respond to the
changes in conditions ahead, so tragedy strikes.

In regard to our own guilts, the remembering comes upon us
unexpectedly. Our hands become clammy and moist, our brow
breaks out in perspiration, a sudden heaviness hits us just behind our breastbone and we might actually utter a groan of
agony. We are remembering.

When we forget, though we might remember the incident men-
tally, the emotional memory is gone. There is no sweaty palm,
no perspiration on the temple, no inward groaning. We are free
of the past to decide on the future.

God desires that we live in a covenant atmosphere of forgetting and forgiving. Life is too short to waste on bad memories and guilt trips of the past.

Moreover, when we are guilty, others can manipulate us through our guilt. Find the guilt in people's lives and you can play them like an organ, getting out of them almost any tune you want. When we are free from the past, no one can manipulate us like that. Our response can be, "The important ones know it all; there is nothing you can hold over my head."

Thank God for His covenant of forgiving and forgetting! What a great way to live!

The Costliness of Covenant

There is one more characteristic of covenant-making. It is seen in our Lord's comments at the table with His disciples on the last night of His earthly ministry before His crucifixion (Luke 22:14-22).

The scene is an Upper Room on the eve of the Passover. Jesus is there with His disciples in a *chaburah*. A variety of emotions fill the air with a mixture of love, expectancy, anxiety, and fear. During the meal, Jesus takes bread, and after giving thanks, He breaks it and says, "Take, eat; this is My body." Then after He has eaten, He lifts the cup and makes an historic statement about covenant. "Drink of it, all of you; for this is My blood of the covenant, which is poured out for many for the forgiveness of sins" (Matthew 26:26-28).

"In My blood which is shed for the payment and removal of your sins." There it is—the costliness of covenant-making. More often than not we think of covenants as warm, fuzzy kinds of experiences where everything is affirmation and love. Seldom do we realize that at times covenants can be agonizingly costly; the pain of disappointment, the burden of energy expended in a long vigil which may not be for a physical illness but rather for a psychological recovery. The cost of working through relational strains with a covenant partner can be exhausting. At times we would rather throw in the towel and walk away to nurse our bruises.

At other times material possessions or finances must be made available to help the foundering friend. Physical limitations may mean suffering inconveniences so that we can minister to our handicapped partner. Sooner or later, we will pay some sort of price for being in a covenant. Such costs should not surprise us nor repulse us. Our Lord made the point very clearly. And what He did, He did with joy. "For the joy that was set before Him, [He] endured the cross, despising the shame . . . (Hebrews 12:2)." He could see ahead to the outcome and so carried through with joy.

I hope this short study of the biblical basis of covenant will serve as a foundation for the chapters which follow. Now, in the hope of discovering some guidelines for covenant relationships, I would like to peruse with you the relationship Christ had with His disciples.

3 Speaking in Love, of Course

The covenant of affirmation: There is nothing you have done or will do that will make me stop loving you. I may not agree with your actions, but I will love you as a person and do all I can to hold you up in God's affirming love.

> And when they came to the place which is called The Skull, there they crucified Him, and the criminals, one on the right and one on the left. And Jesus said, "Father, forgive them; for they know not what they do" (Luke 23:33-34).

Agape love, unconditional love, affirming love—there it was, nailed to the cross and praying a prayer of forgiveness! The world can never understand that love until it experiences that love, because that agape love is not native to mankind. Human love has its limits. Go beyond them, and our love is all over: "We are friends to the bitter end, but this is the bitter end." Not so with Christ. He loves us to the end.

God's love is the basis of covenant groups. "Love knows no limit to its endurance, no end to its trust, no fading of its hope; it can outlast anything. It is, in fact, the one thing that still stands when all else has fallen" (1 Corinthians 13:8, PH). This love has but one source, and that is God Himself. It is not human love; it is the love which comes from God's Spirit, a fruit of His tree. Therefore, without this love of Christ, a covenant group is doomed to tragic limitations.

Admittedly, this goes beyond normal human love. We humans can take only so many hurts before we turn away with our resources depleted. We build walls to protect ourselves from those who wound or disappoint. "But," we protest, "what else can we do? We're only human!"

We Can Follow God's Own Example

Look for a moment at what God did.

We had greatly disappointed God. He had given us the earth with the power and talent to understand it with the idea that we would use our knowledge creatively; we were intended to become a blessing to one another. But that wasn't the way things worked out. We misused our power and tried to enslave one another; we wasted the resources of our earth and destroyed each other's lives. Every time we wounded the creation, we wounded God, because He loved what He had made. He was angry—God has feelings too—and had every reason to turn His back on us. But He didn't. He kept on loving us. He went to the limit of love by sending His own Son to die for our sins.

Only when we allow God's love to flow into us can we love the way He does. Only when we experience how much He loves each one of us can we begin to love another person in the same way. The love I am speaking of is the fruit of God's Spirit, not ours.

How Can I Love You?

There are times when I become so angry with a person that I want to say, "Get lost! You've had it!" That's the natural part of me—the limit of my human love. Then I remember how many times I've done some idiotic thing, the times I've hurt people, or the ways I've misused the creation. Yet, God still loves me. He hasn't crossed me off His list, so how can I cross anybody off *my* list? Can't I see that when a person hurts me, he does it out of his need, his insecurity, or his pain? What good will it do for me to react to his behavior? He needs my love, not my vengeance. He needs some firm ground to stand on, some resources to fill his empty bucket. Something outside of me says, "There's another way to live—keep going back in love."

It isn't easy; it isn't natural to me, and I certainly can't claim the accomplishment for my own, but many times I am able to react in love when ordinarily I would reject in anger. The important thing is that my affirmation makes a difference not only in the life of the person who has hurt me but in my own life as well.

In one of my covenant groups there is a man I will have to encounter one of these days. While claiming to be open-minded, he attacks any opinion that doesn't coincide with his own, and that gets my back up. He has a keen mind and a sharp tongue that can do a lot of damage, especially to people who are already hurting. I'd like to tell him off, to make him aware of what he is doing and saying, but I can't—not yet.

His outbursts of anger are only symptoms of an inner need, and until those needs are met, the symptoms will not disappear. Through encounter, the group or I might bring a stop to this particular set of reactions, but others would replace them. If this man can know love and be assured of an affirmation that will not cease, then there is a chance for him to have the voids of the past filled and the pool of anger pumped dry. There will be no need for him to search for ways to hurt people, because the desire to hurt will have been taken away and replaced with a desire to give, even as he has received. My first job is to love this man; the group feels the same thing. The time will come for this encounter, but now is the time for love.

If You Love Somebody, Tell Him

Affirmation is the most important of all the covenant character-istics, for without it none of the others can function. It forms the basis for which each of us can step out in a new lifestyle.

Most of us spend our lives in a painful awareness of our faults and shortcomings—some of them real and many imagined. We've become a society of nitpickers dedicated to finding out what is wrong with ourselves and others. We are negatively oriented, guilt-weighted, self-deprecating, and taught to analyze critically. We find something wrong with us, and we get stuck thinking about our insufficiencies.

For instance, we have a limp. We find the problem—a shortened leg. So what do we do? Saint Paul has the answer—affirmation. "Whatever is true, whatever is honorable, whatever is just, whatever is pure, whatever is lovely, whatever is gracious, if there is any excellence, if there is anything worthy of praise, think about these things ... and the God of peace will be with you" (Philippians 4:8-9).

So with a shortened leg, you are not going to be the world's fastest runner. That is out. But is that all there is? How about your hands, your mind? You might compose music, paint artistic scenes, develop new chemical formulas, teach children to read, or prepare the kinds of meals and have the home atmosphere where a family can eagerly come together and enjoy the laughter and love that make life worth living. You might listen while somebody pours out a painful story and then give him the encouragement to begin tomorrow with strength. Why get stuck on the shortened leg when there is so much more potential within you?

The covenant of affirmation helps people look at the things of excellence—at those things worthy of praise. No wonder those in the covenant of affirmation feel the peace of God! Give others that kind of love, and they begin to discover who they are and that they are loved for it. They don't have to win false races anymore to get their strokes; such super efforts are only signs of hang-ups. Strokes will come whether or not big races are won; so why run so unnaturally fast? These folks can now settle down to the joy of discovering themselves—because they are in a covenant of affirmation.

In one of the groups a middle-aged man whom I will call

Fred came to his first meeting under obvious emotional stress. Usually it takes a new member a little while to open up and talk comfortably, but this man opened up immediately. He was close to tears as he described what had happened to him. A trusted friend had embezzled from Fred, and as a result, his own business was on the verge of bankruptcy. He blamed himself for the disaster because, though he had made the usual investigation of his friend's credentials, he had not discovered the truth—a con game. Fred had invested his and other people's money. Realizing what the loss would mean to his family and friends, he was in torment.

The surface of Fred's life was a debris of shame, anger, fear, and guilt, but the group didn't respond to that. They responded to his pain. Instead of telling him what he should have done, which he already knew, or theorizing about how to solve his problem, or telling stories of similar problems of their own, they just listened attentively and with concern. Without uttering a single word, they told him, "Fred, we're in this with you." They expressed their love so that he knew he wasn't alone, that he had resources. He had the loving support of his wife and family—and now his covenant brothers. It gave him a secure base from which he could step forth, however shakily, to cope with his difficulties. And he was magnificently free to put his brilliant talents to work in a process of recovery and restitution.

Creating the Atmosphere for Openness
When we agree to love someone unconditionally, we commit ourselves to continue the relationship even in the face of deep personal hurt and disappointment. This means that we have to see the other person as he really is, understanding the deep, unmet needs that can cause bizarre behavior. We have to allow the other person to reveal himself without fear of rejection. Then we create the atmosphere of openness. Naturally, we don't like a lot of what we see, but we have to look past the surface debris to the fundamental needs of his life. This takes time. It also takes restraint, because it is not our job to rebuild the other person's life but to support him as he rebuilds it.

Unconditional love has no escape hatches. It's in there to stay, and both persons in a committed relationship must understand that. Just as God kept renewing His covenant with man, no matter how many times man broke the covenant; we must do likewise in relation to the other person. That doesn't mean we have to humor him or be less than honest with him. We're affirming the *person,* not necessarily approving everything he does. In fact, one of the eight covenant characteristics is that of honesty—the subject of a later chapter.

Four Essentials of Godlike Love

When we love someone the way God loves us, (1) we take the *initiative* in affirming him; (2) we always give the other person a chance to say yes; (3) we don't give up; and (4) we do something constructive.

Take the Inititative

When we love someone unconditionally, we are always ready to take the inititative in order to reconcile our differences. Our love is like the light, which does everything it can to fill the darkness. Sometimes the light may be shut out, for example when a door is closed, but that isn't the light's fault. The moment the door opens or the obstacle is removed, the light instantaneously dispels the darkness.

A woman in our neighborhood was, for all her gentleness, one of the most aggressively loving persons I have ever known. For a long time—for years, in fact—Ann had been slandered by another woman who had once been her friend. Since they knew many of the same people, it must have been embarrassing for Ann to hear from their mutual acquaintances the bitter rumors and gossip her former friend spread about her; yet she never responded in revenge. She kept inviting the other woman back into her life, sensing that the reason for her attacks was her sorrow over her child, who was severely handicapped, and the death of her husband. Ann included the woman in her social life, found reasons to telephone her and ask how she was, and tried to be helpful in any way she could. Eventually, the woman simply had to face the fact that Ann loved her in spite of what she had done. It was then that Ann could tell her, at last, "I know what you have been doing—and I still love you. I don't like the things you've said about me, but that doesn't change the way I feel about you." In time, these two women were reconciled into a lasting, supportive friendship.

Allow the Other Person to Say Yes

Affirming love never holds back, saying: "Oh, she'd never listen anyway!" Love does not presume the response of another, but always gives the other person a chance to respond positively.

An older woman, a senior citizen, joined one of our groups not because she had a specific problem (or so she thought) but because she wanted a close, meaningful relationship with someone. Recently widowed, she felt lonely and inept. She was shy and quiet during the first few meetings she attended. As we learned later, she was convinced that her age made her uninteresting to the younger persons in the group, and she thought her comments and observations were dull. She had been a housewife most of her adult life, and it seemed to her that everyone else in the group was involved in activities and careers that were fascinating by comparison. Usually she began every statement with an apology or a put-down of herself. The group had to draw her out.

Then something began to happen. Boring as she thought her ideas were, she couldn't help noticing that the other members of the group listened to her attentively, even sought her opinion on matters that were important to them. As she began to relax a little, the other members could laugh—not at her but with her—as she told of her experiences. Gradually she sensed that the things she shared were resources to other people. She had a creative mind, a warm interest in people, an appreciation of detail, and an eye for color and composition. One day when she returned home she saw her house as if for the first time. The rooms were artfully arranged and tastefully furnished; her garden, tiny and lovingly tended, was a miniature formal land-scape. Some of her old daydreams about becoming an artist came back to her. Should she give it a try? At her age? Why not!

After trying her hand at a number of art forms, our senior citizen became a photographer of great skill and imagination. One Christmas she had some of her photographs made into cards which she sent to her friends, and several people asked her where they could get some for themselves. She now has a little business of her own, and one of her customers is a greeting-card company. Through their love, her covenant sisters had given her the chance to say yes to the best.

Don't Give Up

Sometimes, when two people are in a covenant relationship, one person opts out. That doesn't mean that the covenant is ended—broken, yes, but renewable.

A coupled married for ten years certainly had grounds for divorce by most people's standards. The husband was an alco-holic who physically and verbally abused his wife and son; yet his wife stayed with him because she believed that somewhere beneath all the pain was a man worth loving. So she held their family together and gave him a firm base from which to carry on his career. It wasn't easy, and there were times when her doubts seemed to get the better of her faith. More than once she confided to her close friends that she was about to give up and leave her husband, and each time she asked them to pray with her to find the strength she needed to make it through each violently uncertain day. But after ten years, it was her husband who gave up—or rather, gave in. Her love and firm honesty got to him, and he joined Alcoholics Anonymous. Eventually he stopped drinking. His entire personality changed, and he be-came the gentle, warmhearted husband and father his wife always believed he could be.

Her love—agape love from God—wouldn't give up. Again, recall the words of the Apostle Paul, "Love knows no limit to its endurance, no end to its trust, no fading of its hope; it can outlast anything. It is, in fact, the one thing that still stands when all else has fallen (1 Corinthians 13:8, PH).

Love Always Looks for a Way to Be Constructive

We learn and we grow much more by affirmation than by criticism. That doesn't mean that we can't encounter persons close to us. They need our honesty—provided they are convinced of our love—and I think they need that in larger proportions.

One of the women of National Presbyterian Church came into my office one day to share a vision she had. "I'd like to finish my undergraduate degree," she said, "and go on to take a pair of master's degrees in theology and counseling."

"What then?" I asked.

"Then I'd like to counsel," she answered.

"Where would you like to do that, in what sort of surrounding?"

"Here at National," was her pert remark. "I'd like to set up a counseling clinic." Her eyes twinkled with excitement.

Her husband, who had just finished an important job with the government, had thought of returning to the West Coast to manage some business holdings they had there; but on hearing of her dream, he decided to be a "sojourner," as he called it, to find a job in Washington so that he could support her in the realization of her God-given dream.

I was impressed with his love that looked for ways of building her up, undergirding her efforts to realize a potential that was longing for development. The result is a counseling clinic in the church. Several other lay persons are following her example in obtaining advanced degrees and providing healing through sound professional techniques and the application of Christ's therapeutic Gospel.

Covenant love always looks for a way of being constructive.

Another example is a man I knew when I was in seminary. His name was Dr. Don Hall, pastor of the Menlo Park Presbyterian Church. He had a lovely wife and a young son. Colleen and I enjoyed visiting them because there was something about Don and his family life that helped people get in touch with themselves.

"Hi ya, Dynamite!" he used to say when his son came home from his paper route. "How'd it go today?" He was truly interested in everything that was going on in his son's life, and the boy knew it. You could tell by the way he'd open up and rap with his father. And as they talked, Don would ask him, "Well, tell me, why did you do it that way? How did you feel about that? Did you like that?" All were questions that encouraged the boy to bring his deepest feelings to the surface so that they could become part of his life. He knew his father loved him.

Don would do the same with Colleen and me, always asking why we made a certain decision. On receiving our answer, he would cock his head to one side and nod in affirmation. "I like that, OK." At times he countered strongly when he disagreed with our decisions, and more than once he was proven correct. Everything about Don and his family was wrapped in constructive love; we were always better people for having been with them. He's gone now, and we miss him terribly, but we carry the memory of a covenant father who said in his style of availability and honesty, "I love you; I want to be your resource." With covenant friends like that we can face life with boldness and confidence.

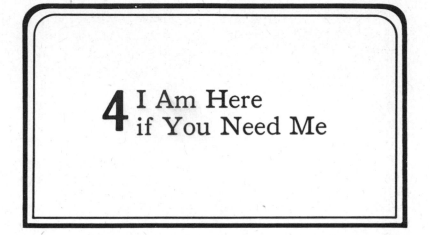

4 I Am Here if You Need Me

The covenant of availability: Anything I have—time, energy, insight, possessions—is at your disposal if you need it to the limit of my resources. I give these to you in a priority of covenant over other noncovenant demands. As part of this availability, I pledge my time on a regular basis, whether in prayer or in an agreed-on meeting time.

And He appointed twelve, to be with Him (Mark 3:14).

"To be with Him." What did Mark mean by that? He had seen something interesting about Christ's relationship with His disciples. Christ had given a priority of presence to His chosen disciples. He loved the crowds; He was committed to be their Saviour; He healed their diseases and enlightened their hungry minds. He was committed to the world.

And yet, He gave a priority of commitment to His disciples. At times He left the crying multitudes on the beach and struck off across the lake in a boat with His disciples. He took them to high places or to the plains where He taught them. They were with Him in a unique and special manner. To them, He trusted His strategy of "chosenness"; in some special way His disciples *were with Him.*

In the covenant of availability, we pledge major portions of what we have and are to our covenant brothers and sisters as they need us. If this is the nature of covenant, then it is quite obvious that we can have only a limited number of covenant relationships. Because of the completeness and uniqueness of the marriage covenant, we have only one wife or husband and only one family. And because of limitations in resources, we can have only a limited number of covenant relationships. Covenants are demanding.

How Do We Make Ourselves Available?

If anyone could have ministered to the whole world, it was Jesus Christ. Yet, He chose to make Himself uniquely available to only twelve persons: "And He appointed twelve, to be *with* Him" (Mark 3:14, italics added), doing His work through them, rather than trying to meet all the needs of the multitudes. He took these men with Him on His teaching missions and on His private retreats; He went to their homes and knew their families. *He gave them Himself; anything He had was available to them*—His ideas, His feelings, His strategies, and His physical and spiritual resources.

One day He was tired after preaching all day. He got into a boat and asked His disciples to row Him across the lake to a quiet place where He could rest, away from the crowds who had been following Him everywhere. But the crowds saw where He was going and ran around the lake to meet Him on the opposite shore. Instead of telling them to go away, Jesus ministered to them, but after they dispersed, He still went off and took His rest.

From His behavior we learn three important things about making ourselves available: (1) we commit our resources to a covenant brother or sister in spite of inconvenience and, at times, great cost; (2) we can commit ourselves in such a way to only a few people; and (3) we must also be committed to ourselves.

Committing Our Resources

All of us have some resources to make available to others, whether they be time, energy, insight, love, or material possessions. We make these available to covenant brothers and sisters as they need them and as we are able.

One of the greatest resources is that of time. We all have the same amount, and it is very precious. Time is the great equalizer of humanity, and each of us determines how he or she will spend it. When we give time to someone, we are giving an irreplaceable resource. That is why we feel so blessed when a busy person, who has many other responsibilities, spends that irreplaceable gift on us.

Children are aware of the covenant of time—or should I say, the lack of it? One of the best things that has come out of the feminist movement is the awareness that it takes more than a mother to bring up a child. Fathers have to make themselves available too. This is what gives a child a sense of security and importance, knowing that he is worth his parents' time rather than being an inconvenience.

In my counseling sessions I talk with many people of all ages who have been brought up with adequate material advantages but sadly inadequate access to the resources of their parents—particularly their fathers' resources of time, energy, conversation, attention, insight, and empathy. It isn't that their parents don't want to give of themselves. They've just been "too busy."

This happens to all of us, at times, but to some of us it becomes a way of life. I've had to cope with this problem in my own life, and fortunately I have a wife and children who call me on it when I become too involved in my work. Generally I try to keep one eye on the dials, so to speak, and if one of the needles shows that someone in my family has a deepening need, I try to be aware of it. But sometimes I don't check the dials often enough. When someone wants to talk, he doesn't get my attention even though I may appear to be listening; too many "urgent" situations may call me from too many family dinners; I'm so busy hurrying from one appointment to another that someone who needs me may feel guilt about bothering me. Yet, I'm in a unique covenant relationship with every member of my family, and they are with me. I need them as much as they need me, and if I'm not making myself available to them, then I'm also not allowing them to be available to me.

The first few times my wife and children encountered me on my busyness, I had to admit that I was running too fast. That's when I had to make a clarification between my primary love for God and my devotion to the ministerial profession. The two were not the same. Because I loved God, I wanted to give my family what He had designed for fathers to give to families. I had to carve out a segment of my time for my wife and children, which meant that I had to carve it out of the professional block. Therefore, if I really loved God, I would give my family what I should, and then I would give to my profession what I could. I find I have more to give to my profession when I enter it as a healthy, invigorated, and resourceful human being. However, when I get going so fast that I don't have time for my wife and my children, I'm not nearly as effective as a pastor and consequently fail in another of my covenant relationships—that with the congregation I serve.

I knew a man who was coming to the same conclusion, but he thought he would have to resign from his job. He had been with a small but rapidly expanding company for several years; he was their fair-haired boy and had a responsible, well-paying position—all of which was hard to give up. But he realized that the job asked too much of him. He was becoming a stranger to his family, and when he was home he had the office on his mind. He loved his job but was losing touch with his family. Vaguely he sensed that there were problems he should be helping to solve, confidences he should be there to share, and moments of fun and relaxation that would bring him close to the persons who meant most to him.

He knew God loved him, and he also knew that his family would back him up, so on that basis he made a moral decision that changed his life. He asked the board chairman for the privilege of speaking to the board. On the appointed day, he stood anxiously before his colleagues and said he could no longer follow a schedule that was tearing his life to pieces. He would have to give a smaller part of his life to his work. His family had to come before the corporation, and if he had to make a choice between them, he would choose his family. Then he expressed his appreciation for his colleagues and for the opportunity they had given him to follow through on his creative ideas. "Gentlemen," he concluded, "if this is not acceptable to you, please accept my resignation. I will leave with a sense of deep gratitude in my heart for having spent these exciting years with you."

He sat down, breathing heavily. The room was deathly still. Everyone was stunned. Then the young president cleared his throat and said, "You know, you've had the courage to say what each of us has been feeling, and I can tell you that from my own personal experience. We just were afraid to admit it."

The resignation was not accepted. Instead, new working guidelines were approved and became company policy. Now no one in that company works after regular office hours or on weekends, except in dire emergencies, which are frowned on. Unnecessary business travel is discouraged, and business is as good as ever. All because one man got his covenants of availability squared away.

Committed to a Limited Number
Jesus chose twelve to be with Him.

"Only twelve? But I thought He was concerned for the *world*!"

He was, but the question is: How does one take what one has and use it most effectively? The answer: By committing oneself to a limited number in covenant relationships.

If being available in covenant means that whatever we have is available to the other, we can say that to only so many people, or we will be torn to shreds. Try to respond to every call in the night and be all things to all people, and there is one result:

exhaustion! When we try to suckle the whole world, we begin to show it physically in the fatigue that concerns those who love us, and show it psychologically in loss of motivation or initiative, in threadbare emotions that pop off with little provocation, in discouragement and cynicism concerning social events, and in a low tolerance threshold. Instead of being part of the solution, we become part of the problem. Sooner or later we have to say no, and that may as well begin with those with whom we are in a covenant relationship.

The counterargument comes flying back: "But doesn't that end up in exclusiveness?"

It can, unless the love we get is healthy enough to turn outward instead of inward. When we are participants in healthy love, which we hope characterizes covenant groups, we desire to reach out and share it, not hold it to ourselves. The covenants are a healthy form of love, not one that excludes out of fear or a sense of superiority, both of which are marks of immaturity.

Even within covenant relationships there are priorities. As far as I am concerned, my principle covenant group is my family. When they say, "Need!" that is where I must respond first. There is only one covenant that comes before family, and that is the covenant with God. He never takes more than His share, and then sends me back into other relationships refreshed and with ample resources.

Each person has to work out his or her priorities, depending on the needs in his or her own life and those of the family. Our four children are close in age, and while they were growing up, Colleen enjoyed her career as a mother. She could have continued her promising career as an actress, but she felt that our family needs and that of starting a new church were all she wanted and could handle comfortably at the time. When our children reached their teens, Colleen felt that their need for her was reduced and also their wants were different; so she was ready to take on a new commitment. She had always wanted to write, and she began to put some of her time aside to work on magazine articles, and then finally a book. The book was a success and others began to follow. Now, as my wife feels less of a need to be available at home, she is more available to the demands of a career. For her it has been a comfortable transition because she was able to shift her priorities as the seasons of her life changed.

I had to do some adjusting myself when I realized that she needed some time for her career. We had always entertained a lot, which was a carry-over from the early days of my ministry when our church was in our home. We loved having a houseful of people having a good time, but it took more of my wife's resources than I had my right to ask. In fact, it was my turn to resource her in her career as she had—and still does—in mine. We still like to entertain, but we do it less frequently and with smaller numbers of people.

After the family comes the commitments in the next echelon of covenant groups and then our business or professional covenants. And believe me, that is enough! If we work these covenants well, we do our share of giving the world what it needs. We have to trust others to do their part and, even if they don't, we can, as individuals, sing only one part at a time; one person can't be a whole chorus.

Getting Enough to Give to Others

When I was growing up as a new Christian, I used to hear this explanation of joy: "Jesus first, others second, and yourself third." I suppose there is some truth to that, but *after* an important filling has taken place. We cannot give out of an empty bucket. We must receive before we have anything to give.

"Love the Lord your God. . . . This is the great and first commandment. And a second is like it, You shall love your neighbor *as* yourself" (Matthew 22:37-39, italics added). That means "in the same manner as." As what? As you love yourself. In other words, if you don't know how to love yourself, how can you know how to love others? Remember the Golden Rule: "Do unto others as you would have them do to you." One has to have some idea of what would feel good before he can do good to another.

Do we know how to love ourselves healthily? Some of us get rather indulgent, I'll admit; that's not what we're talking about.

Love your body.

The body—what a marvelous instrument! It can keep going for the better part of a century with surprisingly little maintenance or repair if given good care. It deserves some reasonably tender care. Exercise keeps the muscles in good tone and improves our circulation. Rest allows the body to rebuild worn-out tissues and recoup expended energy before we draw heavily on the batteries again. The right kind of food builds up but doesn't fatten up. How is your weight? Do you love yourself? How about the habits of intake? How much stuff goes into you and me that we know is bad for us? Why do we do it?

How much do we love ourselves? Too many of us say yes to too many unhealthy things.

Love your mind.

The mind—an amazing computer—but it is more. It can do what a computer can't do: think creatively. But it needs input, time, and new ideas from reading or being in the presence of creative people.

Colleen and I recently had the privilege of visiting two grandchildren of Alexander Graham Bell in their summer home in Beddeck, Nova Scotia where Bell did so much of his experimentation. The grandson, Melville Bell Grosvenor of *National Geographic* magazine, was educated in his early years primarily by his grandfather. What an experience to be in the presence of a creative mind like that during the formative years! And it shows in both Mel Grosvenor and his sister Carol Myer. They are alive with enthusiasm and creative imagination as if the whole of life were in front of them. What a stimulation!

We all cannot be educated by Alexander Graham Bells, but there are exciting people we can choose to be our educators. Many of them lived hundreds or thousands of years ago, but they are still available to us in books. One of the best ways to love our minds is to submit them to strenuous stimuli.

How about our minds? Have we loved them enough to place them in the circumstancs of stimulation?

Not only do minds need stimulating, they need relaxation and recreation. Fallow times are as important as creative times; in fact, the latter cannot exist without the former. Some of the most creative ideas for *National Geographic* have come as a result of Mr. Grosvenor's time aboard his yawl, *The White Mist,* holding a weather helm into a stiff nor'easter. His eyes dance with refreshment as the wind strikes his heavily textured face. A waste of time? Hardly! Look at the results.

For a time I had been going morning, noon, and night, trying to minister in a new community. Discouragement had weighed me down, and I wondered if I could keep going. An elder, who had watched me struggle at the last meeting of the session (the church board) drove me home from the meeting and said, "C'mon Louie, let's get you checked out." What he meant was, "Go ahead and get your flying license; I know how you love it."

Bill Gibbs had built Montgomery Field in San Diego and had a large flying service, complete with a flying school. He kept at me for months but I felt guilty taking the time off and spending the money. After he showed me how it could be done without too heavy a crunch on the budget, I started in. One flight did it. I looked forward to that hour each week. I studied the manuals before going to bed; I lived in the afterglow of a flight for days.

Colleen was concerned about the safety, but Bill was gracious enough to take her up one day and let her see how easy and safe it is. I am not sure she is totally convinced, but she knows how much it means to me; so she releases me and encourages me.

I went through several ratings and now fly for business almost exclusively. The mental stimulation of learning in a field that is so different from my profession—a field I have loved since I was a child—and the combination of physically flying the airplane: the navigation, the instrument work, the communications, and decision-making, all go together to make a recreative experience. When I think I am too busy to take time for recreation, then I'm just too busy. We have learned that the hard way. Now when I get down or the pace is too hard, Coke says, "Honey, why don't you and one of the boys go flying?" A waste of time? No. I still struggle with those guilt feelings, but mildly now, because I know what recreation does for the whole being.

What is your recreation?

Love your spirit.

The spirit is that character of humanity that makes us different from the animals and allows our souls to reach out in spiritual and religious touch with God. To know His love, to feel His affirmation, to experience His forgiveness and cleansing when we've fouled up the waters is not only the fulfillment of our being, but needs some means of expression. To love our spirits is to allow them to vent their joy and excitement in some outward expression.

What is your way? Singing, dancing, loud talking in the woods—how do you express outwardly what is happening in the inner spirit? Do you love your spirit enough to let it "air itself"?

How can we give to others in covenant relationships? By first receiving what we need. This is not selfish; it is a normal and healthy lifestyle.

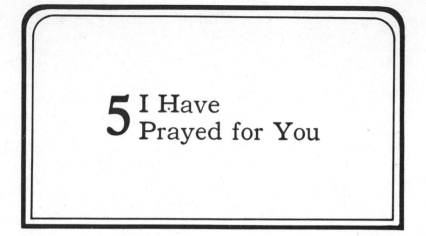

5 I Have Prayed for You

The covenant of prayer: I covenant to pray for you in some regular fashion, believing that our caring Father wishes His children to pray for one another and ask Him for the blessings they need.

> Simon, Simon, behold, Satan demanded to have you, that he might sift you like wheat, but I have prayed for you (Luke 22:31-32).

During the three years of His ministry on earth, Jesus spent months with the disciples, teaching, healing, encountering them, and being His own healthy self in their presence. Who could ask for more?

And yet under certain circumstances Christ felt something more was necessary. He could see Peter wrestling with the ways of doing things. He saw him leaning toward the power tactics, restlessly handling the hilt of his sword as though anxious to use it. When the Sadducees or the Pharisees made their conniving insinuations, Christ noticed the burly fisherman's weather-toughened hands clenching into lethal masses of flesh and bone that could have crushed any of their faces with a well-put punch.

Jesus knew His hefty apostle could be hassled and made to lose control under the right kind of taunting. At times Peter was but a step away from scuttling the kingdom of heaven by his earthy responses. He was overly eager to eat and drink at Christ's table in His kingdom and to sit on a throne, judging the twelve tribes of Israel. Shortcuts were his temptation.

Jesus could see the showdown coming not only for Himself but for Peter. I can imagine the quiet but intense tones in which Jesus caught the attention of the big fisherman: "Simon, Simon, behold, Satan demanded to have you, that he might sift you like wheat, but I have prayed for you" (Luke 22:31-32).

Lately, some theologians have made a great deal out of the doctrine of presence; that is, the importance of our human presence with our fellow humans. In its better forms this doctrine has grown out of our Lord's incarnate life, being God's very presence with us in the form of a human being—a man like the rest of us. But in its weaker moments the doctrine drops back to a base of humanism, implying an essential goodness and sufficiency of humanity to handle its own problems and meet its own needs without any outside help. The result is that the spiritual emphasis of the Christian life, such as prayer or the necessary vine-branch relationship with Jesus Christ, is looked down on and ridiculed as being archaic and obsolete in a world that has come of age. After all, God is dead, and when God in Christ brought the church into being, the church became the focal point of God's presence. When we of the church bring our human presence to bear on a situation, we bring that which mankind can best understand—our humanity.

If anyone's presence would have been sufficient to meet the needs of another human being, it would have been the presence of Jesus Christ! And yet, *He prayed* for Peter! Evidently our Lord brought something more to bear on the situation of Peter's weakness and temptable nature than His own presence.

I am not putting down the need for sensitive, affirming, challenging human presence. We dealt with that in the last chapter. It is crucial; it is right; but it is not sufficient. When we pray for another, we release the grace of God to a loved one in a way that is not possible in any other method of resourcing. In intercessory prayer, God turns loose powers and strengths that are not otherwise available.

I have a cousin named Bob who was in the Army during World War II. He had been in some of Europe's heaviest fighting for several months. One night, my mother woke up with a feeling of deep anguish about him. She just couldn't get him off her mind, and in her concern she got up, knelt by the side of her bed, and began to pray. She prayed for hours until finally her feeling of distress was lifted.

A few weeks later it happened again. Mother woke up thinking about Bob. Something wasn't right. Again, she prayed until the anxiety left her.

Several weeks later Mother got a letter from her sister telling her that Bob had been in two engagements in the Battle of the Bulge and had been wounded on both occasions. He was recovering and would be coming home.

Telepathy? I doubt it. I think God was letting Mother share in the release of His power on Bob's behalf.

Why Do We Pray?

In intercessory prayer we recognize three truths: (1) we are interdependent and responsible for one another; (2) we make God's resources available to others through prayer; and (3) our prayers are answered and the resources flow to those in need.

We Recognize Our Interdependence

In a covenant relationship we pray for others not out of a feeling of superiority—"I don't need anything, thank you, but you do"—but simply because we need each other. Just as the city dweller needs the food the farmer produces, the farmer needs the tractor the city dweller manufactures. Nevertheless, God will not drop bushels of wheat on the city dweller's doorstep if the farmer refuses to produce; nor will He put a tractor in the farmer's field if the factory worker goes on strike. If God did such things, we would become irresponsible overnight. If He withdrew our responsibility to each other, our social structure would totally atrophy.

Perhaps the most oustanding feature of man is not his ability to think abstractly but his ability to relate to another person— to love that person, to accept responsibility for him or her, to work on his or her behalf, and to give strength to that person. When we pray for a covenant partner, we express this ability.

Certain things will not happen in another person's life unless we pray for him. We or a covenant partner may have a need which can be fulfilled only by God's power, and when we pray for someone we love, we make that power available to that person. This is our responsibility to each other.

"But, why doesn't God give us what we need without someone praying for us?" many people have asked. Let's suppose that He did. Suppose God were to give us everything we need without any of us lifting a finger to help each other. What kind of people would we be? Lonely, isolated, uncaring, and uncared for. And God just isn't going to let us go that route. Instead, we were created with the ability to enter into committed relationships in which we provide for each other, and the highest form of provision is prayer.

Making God's Resources Available

A man in one of our covenant groups lost his job unexpectedly when his company went out of business; he came to our meeting almost in tears. Jim was frightened, bewildered, and desperately insecure. When he told the rest of us what had happened and was able to put words around his fears, he began to recover control of himself because he knew that he was not alone. By the next day we would begin helping him look for a new job, we would lend him money to put him through the transition period, and we would give him the moral support he would need to begin over again. But at that moment, while Jim was still in great pain, there was nothing any of us could do for him— except pray. Our own resources were not enough.

"Do you mind if we pray for you?" one person asked.

"No, please," Jim said.

We had no formal way of praying in such a situation. Each member prayed in words that were comfortable for him. Some used few words, others only a word, some prayed eloquently; the variety didn't matter. As the prayers began, we naturally moved toward Jim because we felt close to him; all of us had felt as he was feeling at some time in our lives. Three or four of the men reached out and touched him on the shoulder or hand; there was a great feeling of empathy. Though our situations differed, we were bound by our common need in a beauty of shared relationship.

Gradually the words came; we prayed for peace, for courage, for strength, for patience, and for healing of the hurt. Gradually our brother's shoulders began to relax, his tightly interlaced hands unwound, and he quietly found his brothers' arms. As the prayers ceased, Jim slipped down in his chair to an almost horizontal position, and his tear-filled eyes caught the gaze of each man. Then came a great theological utterance: "Wow!" He stood, raised both fists in the air, and exclaimed, "That's somethin' else!" A few embraces and bear hugs later we took our seats and a kind of silence reigned as we all savored the experience we had just had.

As the weeks wore into months, there were several more times of prayers for our brother with the laying on of hands and prayers for perseverance. Jim made it and claims it was the prayers of the brothers that got him through.

We were not praying out of a sense of superiority or that any of us had what Jim needed. We felt, instead, that God had grace stored up for our friend which would be released as we turned the handles of faith and intercession, allowing God's power to flow. We had the sense of interdependence; we were all in the same boat. We were responsible for one another.

Our Prayers Are Answered and the Resources Flow

A few years ago I made a prayer covenant with a man who was trying to make a difficult business decision that would have a profound effect on his life. Harold was in his late fifties and was forced to make substantial changes in the nature of his business which meant that he would have to risk a lot of his capital in the venture. His business was doing well, and he could have coasted along comfortably until retirement, but he had an idea he wanted to try out. If he went ahead with it and failed, he might lose everything. If he succeeded, he would have something to pass on to his sons.

Harold shared the dilemma with me, and we decided to make a covenant of prayer for several months. From that time on I had little conversation about the affair with him but remembered him regularly in my prayers, praying for wisdom and insight. Finally the answer came to him; he would go ahead with the new idea and take the risk. There were no guarantees, only the secure feeling that he was on the right track, and that made all the difference in the world. Harold went into his new venture with confidence and a sense of assurance which he ascribed to the Lord and our covenant of prayer.

At times, he reported, decisions came down to the last moment, and then the necessary resources were there, as though someone were saying, "It's all right, go ahead." There was no doubt in Harold's mind that the spiritual and emotional strength was given to him day after day, enabling him to stay in the very demanding process. He felt the resources were made available through prayer.

Prayer Covenants

We can make a prayer covenant with anyone who is willing to enter into the agreement. Two people simply agree to pray for each other, not necessarily at any specific time of day, but whenever they pray. The covenant usually is made when one or both partners have a need and require help in coping. The covenant lasts until the problem is solved or the parties feel released from the covenant.

One of my earliest experiences with a prayer covenant was in 1947, shortly after a spiritual awakening had swept through the college department of the Hollywood Presbyterian Church. Among other commitments and disciplines, we accepted the discipline of praying for one another. We formed "prayer triangles" in which two or three would covenant to pray for someone whom they placed in the center of their concern. We had cards printed up so that each of us had a record and reminder of his covenant. There were times when I sensed that some strength was available to me that I could explain only through God's power, and I was convinced that the prayers of covenant partners were responsible for a great deal of the flow.

Since that time I have made many prayer covenants with others and have kept a reminder and record in my loose-leaf datebook marked off into three columns. The first column is for the name of the person or the object of prayer. The second is for the date of entry, and the third for the date of answer. Again and again I have been convinced of the power of intercessory prayer by simply going down the answered column.

Sensitivity to Need

Sometimes both Colleen and I feel a need to pray for someone. Perhaps it is a person with whom we haven't communicated for a long time; yet the need seems urgent. We have learned not to question it but simply to pray. And often it happens that when we meet that person later and tell him how we felt moved to pray for him at a certain time, we learn that it was a time of need or crisis in his life. Though he didn't know we were praying for him, he felt reassured and strengthened.

I'm not sure how, but I do know that when people pray to God, they can also communicate their needs to each other. Through prayer we can ask not only for God's resources but also for the resources of other persons who may not have any other way of knowing we are in need. When you think about it, that isn't so strange; for if God can communicate with each of us—and I believe He can—certainly He can communicate our needs to each other, thereby releasing whatever resources will benefit us.

I experienced this method of communication two years ago when our family was on a backpacking vacation in the High Sierra. Our four children, some of their teenage friends, Coke, and I backpacked twenty-five miles up into the high country from a cabin we had rented. We had agreed that I needed a few days by myself to study and meditate; so when the rest of the troop packed up to go back down the mountain, I remained behind with a small tent, some food, my books, and a great anticipation of enjoying the awesome beauty of the gentle wilderness. I was ready and hungry to rest in the Lord.

After a morning in prayer in which God told me that the first step in His plan for National Presbyterian Church required a sensitive, obedient servant-pastor, I took a day pack up the shoulder of a peak where a lovely small lake was surrounded by a lush meadow of grass and tiny wild flowers that one needed a magnifying glass to see. There I studied, writing an outline of the Epistle to the Romans which I had felt led to preach during the following months. It was one of those creative periods where thought flowed with great ease and clarity.

Toward sunset a quiet thought stole across my mind: "Get back to camp." Wanting to be sensitive and obedient, I started down the hill, stopping for a while, I must admit, to "wet a line" in a small lake that was then in the shadow of the peak as the sun sank. Trout were jumping everywhere! In one hand I carried a spinning rig and in the other, a fly line all ready to go! Now who can resist that? I was surprised that nothing took my lures, as I was sure they would, and on tangling and breaking my favorite gray hackle fly, I sensed again the same instruction: "Get back to camp." "Sorry, Lord," I murmured, donned my pack, and headed down the rugged mountainside over cascades of huge boulders and a rushing stream.

With camp only ten minutes away, a sudden and excruciating pain struck me in the back, at the right side, just above the hipbone. Almost immediately my body began to respond with sweat, trembling, and weakness. I staggered a bit with dizziness. I had to pray for strength just to reach camp. Sick and trembling, I threw off my pack and climbed into my sleeping bag, where for the next ten hours I was in a state of shock. I cried out in prayer for God's healing hand; I sang and repeated Psalm 19 which I had been memorizing that day. I suspected a kidney stone or a gallstone, but I was not enough of a physiologist to know which. Or was it a heart attack? I doubted that.

I needed help, but there was no one in that little isolated valley at ten thousand feet. But how did I know? Maybe some hikers had come up the trailless mountainside and were nearby. Summoning what strength I had, I gave three shrill whistles—a sign of emergency. The whistles echoed back from the face of the mountain, but no one else answered. I looked at my watch; it was almost midnight.

I began to feel weaker; I checked my pulse but could not find any. My hands and feet were numb. Twice my body went into violent spasms which were as disconcerting as the pain was intense.

If only I had some painkiller, but I had none. Maybe, if the pain would subside just a bit, I could find my way down the mountainside with the flashlight. But that was sheer foolishness. It was bad enough finding the trail in daylight over the rocky slopes. I thought of Tim, my second son, who had talked about coming back up after a day or so. Oh, if only he would come back up! It was now 2 A.M.

Then my voice broke and became a low guttural rasp. Just the summer before, I had held dear Bob Brown in my arms at Laity Lodge as he asked us to say the Lord's Prayer while he was slipping away with a heart attack. My voice sounded the same as his. Was this the end? I honestly thought so. "Two or three minutes," I thought, "then it will be all over." I felt no panic; instead a flood of thanksgiving for Coke and the kids.

Then my covenant brothers in Los Angeles came to my mind, and I prayed for them and my brothers in covenant in the Washington prayer group. I thought of my two successors, Donn Moomaw at Bel Air and Hap Brahams at La Jolla—oh, how I loved them!

My mind turned to Tim again. If only he could get the message concerning my plight.

It was then that my mind turned to a number of occasions during our life together when Coke had become aware of my need, though separated by a long distance. She is a woman of wonderful sensitivity to the Lord, and I felt He could get through to her and let her know my problem. I prayed and asked Him to tell her to send Tim up to meet me.

About 6 A.M. the shuddering ceased; the pain seemed to be moving across my back and then finally ceased except for a dull ache. The shock reaction yielded to normal pulse, and I began to feel stronger. I waited until about 7, when the light was full, then got up on shaky legs and started down the hill with just an emergency pack in case the attack came on again. I left behind the remainder of the gear that I knew the kids could come up and get. Checking my pulse frequently, I slowly worked my way down, feeling better all the time. As I reached a winding road, a delightful young couple picked me up and dropped me off at the driveway of our cabin in the foothills. Tim was there, and taking one look at me, said, "Dad, what happened to you?"

"What do you mean?" I asked.

"Your face—your eyes?"

Then I told him the story.

"Strange," he commented. "Just this morning Mom said that she had awakened during the night—about 2 A.M.—and couldn't sleep. She thought maybe I'd better go up the mountain after daybreak to see how you were. I was getting ready to leave."

He looked at me with eyes of deep spiritual understanding, and I couldn't help but embrace him for his readiness and sensitivity.

God can make us aware of others' needs and release His

strength to us. I knew amazing peace and control during the experience. I was very much aware of my loneliness and yet felt deeply God's presence and peace. I was in His hands. I believe it was Colleen's prayers that made available to me the strength I desperately needed.

How powerful these words, "But I have prayed for you."

6 I Need You

The covenant of openness: I promise to strive to become a more open person, disclosing my feelings, my struggles, my joys, and my hurts to you as well as I am able. The degree to which I do so implies that I cannot make it without you, that I trust you with my problems and my dreams, and that I need you. This is to affirm your worth to me as a person. In other words, I need you!

So He came to a city of Samaria, called Sychar, near the field that Jacob gave to his son Joseph. Jacob's well was there, and so Jesus, wearied as He was with His journey, sat down beside the well. . . . His disciples had gone away into the city to buy food (John 4:5-6, 8).

We think of this story as the woman at the well. Christ's warm honesty brought her to the thrilling experience of belief. But have we ever seen another side of the story—that of Jesus' need for His disciples? Somehow Jesus communicated His need for the ministry of the disciples. He let them know He was too tired to go to buy the food. I don't know whether Christ volunteered the information, saying, "Men, I've had it. How about going into town and getting the food?" or whether one of them, sensitive to His condition, said, "Master, you're tired; why don't we go into town and get the food? You rest here by the well." And Jesus agreed.

Whichever way, Jesus admitted His need. He said in effect, "I need you."

The night of His betrayal, Jesus was deeply burdened about His impending death and said to three of His men, "My soul is very sorrowful, even to death; remain here, and watch" (Matthew 26:38; Mark 14:34). Jesus was telling His beloved companions, "I need you."

One of the most difficult things we are called to say in our Christian life is, "I need you." Our society has taught us to be self-sufficient and rugged in our individuality. The covenant of openness is one of the most difficult for us.

In one of our churches a circle of older women had been meeting for fifteen years. They showed some interest in covenant groups, though it was mostly curiosity with much criticism and reservation. They asked me a lot of questions about the subject as we met one day for the monthly Bible study. Having heard several answers, there was general agreement that this kind of group was not for them.

"Why not?" I asked.

"I can't speak for the rest of us," one woman said, "but in my case, I was brought up to keep my problems to myself. To open up my life in such a way would be—well, it would be a sign of weakness."

"It's been the same with me," another woman said. "After all, who cares about our problems? Oh, perhaps we might discuss something personal with a few close friends, but, even then, that isn't why we get together."

The other women agreed. They all had been brought up in much the same way.

"How do you feel about that?" I asked.

"About what?"

"About that kind of cultural conditioning? That stiff-upper-lip, don't wear-your-heart-on-your-sleeve, I can-take-care-of-myself sort of thing?"

I thought perhaps I had probed a little too far and expected a sharp retort. But the woman who had spoken first said, "It leaves me very lonely."

Her openness did something to the others, and within a few minutes they were sharing their inner struggles. One woman said, "I wish I could talk over some of these things with somebody." Another said, "I've carried some burdens for years, and nobody ever knew about them."

"Tell me," I asked the first woman, "what would be necessary before you could talk about your hopes and disappointments—your deepest feelings—with another person?"

She thought for a moment, then stated it beautifully: "I think I would have to be able to trust the other person." They all nodded in agreement.

Then a woman who had recently lost her husband began to talk about her loneliness, and it was interesting to see the reactions of the others as she began to reveal her emotional pain. One or two were embarrassed by it; the others moved their chairs closer to her. As she began to cry, a few put their arms around her.

These women had been meeting in the church for fifteen years and only now were they beginning to include each other in their lives. In one hour they were well on their way to becoming a loving, caring family of human beings who could actually feel God's love moving through them. They were experiencing the covenant characteristic of openness. In short, they were admitting, "I need you."

Admit It

Before we can enter into a close relationship with another person, we have to become aware of our need for that person, which means that we have to acknowledge the fact that we can't make it in this world on our own. For most of us, this is very difficult to do because in our society we are taught to be, or to appear, self-sufficient. We're not supposed to share our problems or admit that we've been hurt because strong people aren't supposed to have any problems. The corollary is that if we do expose a need or a wound, we are weak.

Exactly what is a need? Frankly, it *is* a weakness; it is a quality or an ability we don't have or don't have enough of. Call it a deficiency, if you prefer, and you'll be absolutely correct. But there are two kinds of human weaknesses: those that are built into us and those that are imposed.

God did not create us to be self-sufficient for the simple reason that if we didn't need one another, we wouldn't have anything to do with one another—and we wouldn't go very far if we all had to do everything ourselves. Instead, God designed us with built-in weaknesses as well as strengths, so that we would become interdependent. This common need becomes the basis for human relationships.

Imposed weaknesses are the results of traumas and distortions caused by our own misdeeds and by the impact of other people's lives on us. They destroy our abilities, fill our lives with debris and pain, and urge us to manipulate rather than relate to other people.

God is not about to remake us and eliminate the created weaknesses that bind us together—and to Him. But He does want to heal the distortions caused by our mistakes or those society has imposed on us, and He is quite able to do this, at times, through committed relationships.

If there were any person who didn't need anybody, it was Jesus Christ. Yet in several instances He admitted His need so that His disciples could help Him. And toward the end of His life, when He was wrestling with the knowledge of His impending death, He said in effect to three of his disciples, "Come pray with Me because My heart is heavy" (Matthew 26:37). He needed their presence, and even though they disappointed Him and fell asleep, the point is that He asked them. He was open with them concerning His need. He admitted it, strong though He was.

It is the weak who say, "I don't need you." They simply try

to appear strong when actually they are not. That kind of "strength" is a cover-up.

Keeping Love Alive

In a covenant relationship there is no one person who is always the dispenser or the receiver of love. All give and receive according to their needs. The important thing is that their love continually passes back and forth between them, which is what keeps love alive. For live itself is organic. It is like a plant that receives light, moisture, and carbon dioxide from its environment, then gives back oxygen and moisture. If any part of the process is stalled, the plant eventually dies, and the same is true of love. To replenish itself, it must be used.

When we say, "I love you" to another person it means: (1) we trust that person enough so that (2) we can admit our own needs, (3) acknowledge the strengths of the other person, and (4) include that person in our lives.

These are four things I used to find hard to do. Until several years ago I couldn't be open about my needs because I didn't want to admit that I had any. Colleen was the one who first convinced me that openness was crucial to a relationship, and it took her a long time. Every now and then during the early years of our marriage, she would say, "Honey, sometimes I just don't feel as if you need me." I needed her, all right, but, because I had to play the strong guy, I couldn't communicate it. In those days I was trying to achieve too much and then feeling like a failure because I couldn't reach my goals. So I was looking for a lot of affirmation to fill that huge not-OK void in me, and as much as I longed for Colleen's strength and support, I couldn't put it into words.

Early in Colleen's life her mother and father were divorced, and like most children from broken homes, she felt traces of rejection and insecurity. Though she had learned to recognize them, it was important for her to know that she was needed. Consequently, my inability to express my needs—or to admit that Colleen's strengths were fulfilling them—caused some difficulties for both of us.

Openness about our feelings, the hurts as well as the happinesses, is crucial to a covenant relationship because anything less than that can be interpreted as a rejection. If you and I have a warm relationship, and you see me hurting, yet each time you ask, "Lou, what's the problem?" I try to hide it; this communicates to you that I don't trust you or that there really isn't anything you can do to help me. I'm telling you I don't need you, which is a strong form of rejection. It puts you completely outside of my life.

You might respond nonchalantly by thinking, "Well, that's the way our society is—we just don't share our problems with one another." But I think something deep inside you would say, "I'd love to help you, my friend, and I think I might have something you need, but you won't let me." And rightfully you would be angry because you would feel unimportant to me. Obviously we wouldn't be able to have a close relationship with this kind of barrier between us.

I began to understand how Colleen felt, because once I thought about it, I realized what it was to feel excluded. In an intimate relationship like a marriage, if one person is hurting and doesn't say why, the other person starts trying to guess: "Is it my fault? Have I done something wrong?" Whenever my wife was quiet and troubled, it never occurred to me that she might be thinking her way through a problem. I was sure it was my fault, somehow, and I became very defensive. Yet by my self-sufficient attitude, I gave her frequent cause to feel that way.

In my staff relationships I also had some difficulties because I couldn't say, "I need you people." Of course, in a way I was telling people I needed them when I asked them to work on certain projects. But all too often I was taking the responsibility back by running around and doing the job myself before they could get started. I might just as well have said, "I don't trust you to do your thing," because that's the message they got.

It took me a long time to convince people I needed them after I realized it myself. At first the words didn't come easily, and then I was shocked when nobody responded. In fact, for about a year and a half, all I saw, whenever I said "I need you" to anyone were the soles of his shoes going over the bushes. My facade of self-sufficiency had been *that* impressive. But finally people began coming back with a funny little smile on their faces. "Do you really mean that?" some of them would ask.

"I sure do."

"Well, maybe I've got something that can help you."

That was when I discovered what it was to have close relationships. I got presentations of love that I had never known before as people came into my life with their strengths. I had been very shy and looked at people as intrusions on my privacy. Now I saw them as delights. I needed them, and if that was a weakness, I thanked God for it.

One of the things that will shut down a covenant group immediately is when one member has a need and won't share it. Somehow the group always senses it, and the disappointment runs deep. What the "Oh, no, everything's OK" really says is: "You don't have anything I want." That's a big put-down.

Not long ago I learned what it was to be on the outside of someone's life, wanting most eagerly to be allowed in. One of my sons was going through the "ionization" period of the teenage years—which I compare to that time when the astronauts reenter the atmosphere and experience a temporary blackout, making communication with them impossible. Actually our relationship was maturing as it grew into a new phase, but during this ionization time, our inability to communiate with each other made me feel rejected. I longed for some contact with my son but knew I had to wait until he got in touch with me. That took about a year and a half.

Then one day my son said, "Hey, Dad, I want to talk to you. I've got something I need to ask you. Got a few minutes?" It was obvious that something heavy was coming along—and I was very much up for it. My son and I were talking again!

We found a place where we could speak privately, and I listened while my son told me about something he wanted very much to do. He had enough money put aside to get him part of the way toward his goal, and he said to me, "Dad, I need some bread. Will you help me?"

I almost went through the ceiling with joy as the pattern of silence and rejection was broken, and he asked me for something that I could give. He wanted me to lend him the rest of the money he needed and had worked out a plan by which he could pay it back.

When my son paid me back, right on time, it gave him a sense of personal pride and independence. But in needing me, he affirmed me. He gave me a chance to resource him, to liberate him to the greater use of *his* resources. By including me in his life as a covenant partner, he made me feel that I was *somebody*. He had said, "I need you."

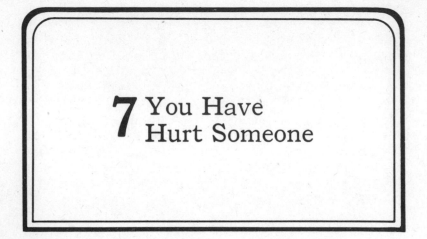

7 You Have Hurt Someone

The covenant of honesty: I will try to mirror back to you what I am hearing you say and feel. If this means risking pain for either of us, I will trust our relationship enough to take that risk, realizing it is in "speaking the truth in love" that we grow up in every way into Christ who is the head (Ephesians 4:15). I will try to express this honesty in a sensitive and controlled manner and to meter it, according to what I perceive the circumstances to be.

> Jesus said to Simon Peter, "Simon, son of John, do you love Me more than these?" ... He said to him the third time, "Simon, son of John, do you love Me?" Peter was grieved because He said to him the third time, "Do you love Me?" (John 21:15-17).

Can you and I imagine the pain Peter must have felt after denying Christ three times? He had boldly affirmed his love and loyalty even though others might go against Christ. Yet, when the showdown came, he denied Him three times and swore that he never knew Him. So deep was Peter's grief that he went out and wept bitterly.

Until Peter could work that out with Christ, he would be dogged by shame and guilt, and among the other disciples he would be the butt of ridicule: "Peter the Rock, ha!"

After the Resurrection, Jesus saw the disciples fishing, and when they had come ashore and eaten the barbecued fish Jesus had prepared, He asked Peter three times if he loved Him. Embarrassed, Peter said yes, but he and everyone else knew his love had fallen short. It was painful that Jesus asked him three times, "Do you love Me?" And yet Christ had to face Peter with his denial before there could be any reconciliation. When it was all over, Peter was forgiven and still had his place in the ranks of the disciples.

Before I Tell You the Truth

We have little right to confront a person unless, like Jesus, we: (1) love the person, (2) are sensitive to his ability to receive the truth, and (3) are willing to continue the relationship as he works out his problem.

I remember the first time I was confronted in this way. It happened when I was young and overzealous to the point of arrogance. I wanted so much for others to have the spiritual experience I felt I had, that I encountered everyone on everything I thought was wrong. I spoke the truth—and nothing else; there was no love in what I said. The results were disastrous. I was president of our church college department at the time, and suddenly executive board members began quitting right and left. Even my college roommate, a friend I had known all through high school, became alienated.

One day a man I knew well, the advisor to the college department, sat me down and had a talk with me. Because I knew he loved me, I could accept the truth from him. He was firm, yet kind, as he told me that the way to stimulate enthusiasm was not to make heavy demands on people and then write them cutting letters when they fell short of them—which I had done. This, he explained, was why some were quitting.

I had been completely unaware of what I had been doing, and

even though I still didn't comprehend it all, I began to realize that I had a problem: it wasn't the lack of other people's commitment; it was my judgmental managerial style. The truth hurt, but because this man had offered it to me in an attitude of love, I saw I had done wrong. I felt ashamed but not rejected, and I felt secure in his presence. He knew how much of the truth I could handle, and not once did he allow himself to use a word or an expression that would have put me down. He saw beneath my arrogance to something of which I was not aware—my insecurity—and his faith in me gave me the confidence to look for more loving ways to communicate my hopes and dreams.

Healers of One Another

I learn slowly, it seems, and once again some years ago someone had to speak the truth in love to me about the way I was communicating with people. A member of our church board invited me out to lunch one day and when we had reached a comfortable point in our meal, he told me that some of my staff members are pretty unhappy about the way I was handling things. I would give them responsibility and then take it back, and no sooner would we finish one project than I would be ready to begin another. We never stopped to enjoy the work we had done—never had moments of relaxation together. I made suggestions that, to my staff, seemed like mandates, and I neglected to communicate a feeling of appreciation for their good work.

I couldn't believe this man had his facts straight. As far as I knew, my staff was happy. We worked hard and well, and we were making progress. From time to time I would ask them if everything was all right, and the answer always was: "Sure."

A few months later the same man took me out to lunch again and told me the problem still existed. *OK*, I thought, *I'll prove to him how wrong he is.* I invited him to attend our next weekly staff meeting to see for himself.

Just before the meeting I asked the staff if there were any problems. I even suggested some possibilities. Again: "Everything's OK."

Our board member arrived; the meeting began, and five minutes later he had the lid off the box. I couldn't believe what was coming out of it. The staff began admitting their hostility, their frustration, and their feeling that they simply didn't matter to me.

When the meeting ended I stayed behind, almost shattered. For a moment I sat, staring, and then I put my head down on the desk and let it all come out. I thought I was alone and didn't know the board member had come back into the room until I felt his hand on my shoulder. I was embarrassed to let him see me that way, but much as the truth had hurt, I wanted to thank him for what he had done. And when I lifted my head to look at him, I saw tears in his eyes too. Then he embraced me and said, "Louie, I love you."

During the next few days, I began to see my behavior in a different, more objective light; I remembered that my father also had been a hardworking, hard-driving minister; yet he never had these problems with his staff. That was because he took time out to have some fun with them. When a program was launched or a project completed, my dad, the staff, and all our families would get together for a picnic in the country or an evening of music. I never did anything like that with the men and women who worked with me because I felt uncomfortable about taking any time off from my work. Obviously, I had a lot more to learn from Dad.

At our next staff meeting I tried to be as honest with the staff as the board member had been with me. "Listen," I said, "I have to be what I am—but if, in my aggressiveness, I hurt any of you, I want you to tell me about it so I can get clues and won't let these things go on. I need your strength, so be honest with me." We had a session of honesty and love with each of us stating exactly what he or she felt, and that was the beginning of a totally new relationship for all of us. More and more I began to trust in the capabilities of the men and women who worked with me. I attended fewer meetings. If I made a suggestion in an authoritative tone, someone called me on it. If I stepped in and tried to do a person's job, he reminded me that it was his responsibility. Finally, with the help of their loving honesty, I was able to break out of the prison of over-responsibility and overachievement in which I had lived a good part of my life.

Often we are unaware of the ways in which we may hurt someone. Only through the eyes of another can we get an honest look at ourselves—and how fortunate we are when those eyes also look on us with love.

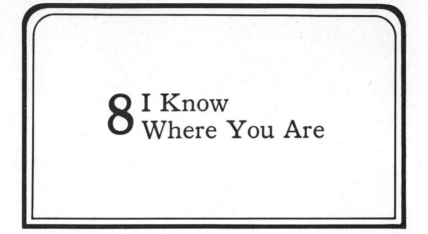

8 I Know Where You Are

The covenant of sensitivity: Even as I desire to be known and understood by you, I covenant to be sensitive to you and to your needs to the best of my ability. I will try to hear you, see you, and feel where you are and to draw you out of the pit of discouragement or withdrawal.

And behold, a woman of the city, who was a sinner, when she learned that He was sitting at table in the Pharisee's house, brought an alabaster flask of ointment, and standing behind Him at His feet, weeping, she began to wet His feet with tears, and wiped them with the hair of her head. . . . Now when the Pharisee who had invited Him saw it, he said to himself, "If this man were a prophet, He would have known who and what sort of woman this is who is touching Him, for she is a sinner." . . . And He [Jesus] said to her, "Your sins are forgiven" (Luke 7:37-39, 48).

She had followed Jesus into the den of judgment. The house of a Pharisee was no place for a woman of the streets! In spite of knowing that she would receive severe judgment from the

Pharisees, she went anyway. What could have drawn her into such a situation?

We get a clue from the behavior of Jesus. And yet He seems to do nothing. But look for a moment. She is standing behind Him, wetting His feet with her tears. She sees what is happening and stoops down to wipe her tears from His feet with the only thing she has available, the long hair which flowed down past her shoulders—the mark of her trade. (No decent woman would let her hair down!) While accomplishing this, she begins to kiss His feet! Why?

Believe me, if some beautiful woman with a reputation were to do those things to me, I would probably pull my feet away in embarrassment, being unable to handle such a demonstration. But not Jesus. He accepted her actions without embarrassment, and this touched her deeply. She knew that as a harlot she would make anyone else unclean. And yet He didn't seem to mind. She felt so much understanding that she kissed His feet and then anointed them with an expensive perfume—and you can imagine where she got that!

Speaking to the Pharisee, Jesus recognized her need, saying, "She loved much" (Luke 7:47). Searching for love, she had tried to find it in self-defeating ways. Jesus was not nearly as concerned with her self-defeating ways as He was with her inner need. He met that need with loving acceptance and an understanding of what she was doing. She went away cleansed and filled.

I Feel Your Pain

Bill had been quiet during most of the group's weekend meeting. Only twice during the first night did he mention what was on his mind, but we failed to follow it up with sensitive response.

We were a covenant group of ministers, meeting to talk over some professional problems. The one we kept coming back to was the matter of housing: should we live cost free in a house provided by the congregation, or should we buy a house like anyone else? More and more of us were opting to own our homes so that we could be a part of the financial community and have a place to live as responsible citizens when we retired. We had known older, retired ministers whose pensions could provide for their families' food and clothing but not for their shelter. Each of us knew how many times, in our own congregation, a special offering had been taken to help these people.

It was a sticky problem. Some ministers wanted to own their homes; some didn't. Some church boards went along with the idea, which implied a housing allowance for ministers, and some opposed it.

What our group didn't sense that weekend was that the quiet member among us was coming up against this problem in his own life. Called to a new church, Bill had to make a decision about buying a house or living in the manse. His church board was considering these alternatives with a good deal of tension, and he had to decide how to approach them on it. Hoping to share his feelings with us and possibly get some feedback, he started twice to describe his personal situation, but somehow our attention went off in a generalized discussion of the subject.

"Oh, sure, I know how you feel. Just the other day I was saying. . . ."

"A friend of mine has the same problem. Hey, I ought to get in touch with him—a real sharp guy."

"That must be tough. I suppose a lot of us are going to come up against the same situation."

That sort of thing.

The covenant of sensitivity at that moment was not operating in our group. We had let our covenant brother down.

At our last session before leaving for home, one of us said to our quiet member, "Say, Bill, you haven't said a word all weekend. How come?"

Bill's face reddened. In a burst of anger he said, "I can't share anything with you guys! More than once I tried to tell you I was hurting; twice I put up my distress flag, and you ignored it!"

How often that happens to each of us almost every day. We

have a pain—maybe a small one, maybe it's pretty big—and we want to ease it by telling someone about it. Maybe if we can hold it at arm's length and get some perspective on it, we'll begin to figure out what to do about it so it won't hurt so much. The people we know keep coming up to us, putting a hand on our shoulder or grasping our hand in theirs and saying, "Hi, how ya doing?" But it really isn't a question, and they really don't want to know the answer. "Hey, you look great!" they tell us without actually looking and go on their way without seeing pain that throbs just below the surface of our faint, wan smile.

Most of the group shuffled uncomfortably.

"OK," one man said, "we're sorry you feel this way, Bill, but I guess that's your privilege."

Then somebody else said, "Wait a minute. We've got a hurting brother. We failed him, and we can't leave without coming to grips with that."

We all knew he was right, and we apologized to Bill for our insensitiveness. We remained with him for the rest of the morning, and this time, when he talked about the particulars of his problem, we listened not only with our ears but with our committed love. We began to feel what was going on inside him. We knew the urgency of his situation; we explored with him alternative solutions. By the time we all left for home, Bill knew what he was going to do. We had displayed a classic example of insensitivity, but thank God, we had seen it in time to make amends.

When we wave a flag of trouble and our loved ones go past without stopping, it makes us angry—and rightly so. We feel rejected, disappointed, unimportant, and it doesn't take many of those experiences to make us decide, "If that's the way they feel about me, I'll take care of it myself!" And so we withdraw.

Managing Our Relationship Resources

Sensitivity takes up space in our lives. It can also be crowded out. If we string ourselves out, expending 100 percent of our time and energy, there is no way in which we can adjust to the unexpected emergency. If we drive ourselves to the point of saturation—and beyond—with professional, community, or social pursuits, we cannot possibly be in a sensitive covenant relationship with another person.

We hide behind our newspaper, exhausted, when a wife, a husband, or a child approaches us in need of comfort, understanding, or reassurance. To a tentative, feeble cry for help, we answer with a muttered, "Hey, don't bother me now. Can't you see I'm reading the paper!" We become defensive about our expended energies because there isn't anything left to give. Having nothing in reserve, we tune out the need. The husband, wife, or the child turns away and eventually stops approaching us at all.

In a covenant relationship we must reserve enough energy so that when the person close to us is hurting, we can tune in. When we don't have the resources for sensitivity, something happens to the relationship. Just as in our finances, if we are wise managers, we put aside some of our income for the time when we may lose our job, or face a medical emergency, or a major repair to the house or the car. So we can put aside a certain amount of time and energy for the unexpected human need. And we don't touch that. It becomes a receptive part of ourselves—an available reserve. Having something to give, we can then keep ourselves open to the silent cry of distress.

Just Listen, That's All

I used to get uptight about my preaching. I wanted my sermons to carry a message that would feed the congregation's needs, but I also wanted my sermons to be artfully presented. Usually I felt I didn't have time to give enough attention to my syntax, grammar, metaphors, and phrasing. I have heard some preachers whose sermons were so well organized that, while I wasn't conscious of the way in which they had done it, their messages broke through my walls of resistance and came slamming through to my mind with all the drama, insight, and emotion they were meant to have. That was my unreached goal.

Several times I mentioned how I felt in one of my covenant

groups, and their response was always: "Oh, don't worry about it! Whatever you're doing is great. Just keep doing it."

That was like telling me that I don't have a problem at all. They were getting the message of my sermons, all right, but they weren't sensitive to my inner struggle, even when I put it into words. I was angry because they didn't take my struggle seriously and were judging my feelings according to some criteria of their own. In a way they were telling me to stop behaving like a little boy. Well, maybe I *was* a little boy, but I still had a problem. I wanted to work it out, not gloss over it.

When someone puts up a distress signal, that doesn't mean we have to step in and solve his or her problem. All we have to do is be aware that the problem exists and listen for the sound of pain. "Wait, what was that you said? How do you feel about that?" can do a lot to help another person get his problem out in the open. Then *he* can do something about it.

Where's the Pain?

In our covenant groups we find that we can easily become unresponsive to another person's inner feelings if we allow ourselves to discuss generalities. Or, when someone mentions an experience, we counter with one of our own. Sometimes we have to remind ourselves to speak personally and to draw another person out when we sense there is something going on deep inside.

In one of our meetings we had just reminded ourselves to stop going off on tangents when we began to log in—which is when each member brings the group up-to-date on where he or she is. Then one of our group, a man named Steve, stated quite matter-of-factly that during the week his father had died. A prominent government official, Steve was quiet, intellectual, exceedingly capable but not very communicative about his personal life, (though he wanted to be) and committed to the covenant concept. He had had a wonderful relationship with his father; yet he announced the fact of his death as if everything was OK—until one of the other men in the group said, "Steve, where's the pain?"

All of a sudden the emotion welled up in Steve's eyes and

tears rolled down his cheeks as the group dropped into silence. The group was patient, sensitive, and unembarrassed. Through his tears Steve said, "Hang with me for a minute, will you?" With a few little sounds and some body language, the group gave him the permission to let go.

A few minutes later Steve told us some of his feelings about his relationship with his father. Steve was a person with superior organizational abilities. Because he could see things so clearly, he was in charge of one of the major departments of the government, but whenever things go heavy he would talk them out with his father, either by phone or when he went to visit the old man. His father was a relatively uneducated man; yet he had a native intelligence and wisdom not sharpened by great amounts of education or a sophisticated position. There was an earthiness and realism about him which, to his son, was like a perfect wall against which he could bounce his ideas.

As Steve opened up, he was able to admit how much he was going to miss his father—the counsel, the talks, the quiet love which that man gave him. Sensing the void in his life, the group made themselves available not as a substitute but as a resource. One of our group asked him if we could pray for him, and he said yes.

"We'd just like to lay our hands on you. Would that be all right?"

"Yes."

Steve put his chair in the center of the group, and the rest of us gathered around him, placing our hands on his head and shoulders. In short phrases, we focused our prayers on him, giving him our love and affirmation and calling on God's resources to come into his life. It was a moment of covenant sensitivity. Not only had our group sensed this man's need to talk about his loss—and in doing so to overcome his own personal characteristic of reticence—but we had sensed the gap which his father's death had left in his life. And in some strange and partial way, we stepped into that gap.

Somebody saw Steve's signal. Somebody had his sensitivity receiver turned up high.

9 You Can Trust Me

The covenant of confidentiality: I will promise to keep whatever is shared within the confines of the group in order to provide the atmosphere of openness.

When Jesus had thus spoken, He was troubled in spirit, and testified, "Truly, truly, I say to you, one of you will betray Me." The disciples looked at one another, uncertain of whom He spoke. One of His disciples, whom Jesus loved, was lying close to the breast of Jesus; so Simon Peter beckoned to him and said, "Tell us who it is of whom He speaks." So lying thus, close to the breast of Jesus, he said to Him, "Lord, who is it?" Jesus answered, "It is he to whom I shall give this morsel when I have dipped it." So when He had dipped the morsel, He gave it to Judas. . . . Jesus said to him, "What you are going to do, do quickly." Now no one at the table knew why He said this to him. Some thought that, because Judas had the money box, Jesus was telling him, "Buy what we need for the feast"; or, that he should give something to the poor (John 13:21-29).

Jesus' love covered Judas' sin. All were deeply interested and concerned about who would deny Him. Yet, even before that intimate group, Jesus did not placard Judas' sin but in love kept it as confidential information, except for the disciple whom He loved, probably John.

Jesus saw no reason why this information would help anybody. He knew what Judas had to do, and already this man was under tremendous tension. He was ready to betray the One he had loved and followed for three years—probably caught in the struggle between his fervent nationalism and his love for Jesus, who was disappointing him in not being the kind of Messiah Judas thought He should be. But Jesus kept the face of the coming betrayal so completely to Himself that only one of the other disciples knew what was going on. Jesus exercised the covenant of confidentiality with Judas.

In one of our covenant groups a woman spoke openly about some difficulties she was experiencing in her work. A friend, who also was in the group, was so concerned for her that he went home and told his wife about her. His wife also was a friend of the woman, and when speaking to her on the phone the next day, she ended the conversation by saying, "We're thinking about you a lot and praying everything works out right at the office."

That did it.

The woman felt she could no longer trust the group and left it. The man, when he was encountered by the other members, went through a traumatic experience. At first he couldn't understand what he had done wrong. Finally he realized that the characteristic of confidentiality means that *anything* shared in a covenant relationship goes no farther. This man had told his wife, and even though she was a friend of the woman involved, she was outside the group. A confidence had been betrayed.

In a committed relationship, each person must know that whatever he or she says will be treated as a confidence. Each person must be able to trust the other with personal information. How else can the group be open and honest?

Somebody Leaked!

In our post-Watergate society, the digging out of human error is becoming a way of life. Somebody leaks information given in the strictest confidence, and a mistake, a blunder, or a wrong is exposed for all the world to see.

There are times when a society—or a relationship—needs the exposure of error. If its purpose is constructive, if it is done to help the person involved or to serve justice, then it can be redemptive. But if it is exposure for exposure's sake, if it undresses a person and leaves him naked in the public square to be ridiculed and scorned, then it serves no good purpose. So many confidences are betrayed for this latter purpose that the information leak is becoming a major source of concern. If we tell ourselves that we are acting "for the good of society" when actually we are building our own reputations on the body of a broken opponent, then any justice coming out of such an exposure is only a secondary coincidence. Where there is no love, there is no healing.

Love Covers Up

What do we do when someone close to us confesses a weakness or a mistake or perhaps even a sin? If we love that person and are in a covenant relationship with him, we don't broadcast the information. We guard that person's weakness; our love covers it up.

Jesus Christ had a wonderful day of guarding the weakness of another when it was right to do so. He knew that Judas was going to betray Him; yet the only person He told was John, His best friend. Jesus was too concerned about Judas to expose him to the hostility of the other disciples. He knew what a terrible struggle was going on inside the man and wanted to give him every chance to work it out.

Our love *can* cover a multitude of sins, but when is it right and when is it wrong to do so? Where do we draw the line between the invalid and the valid cover-up?

The Unhealthy Silence

When we cover a person's error so that the wrong can go undetected, when we make no attempt to come to grips with the problem, then we are not guarding a weakness but rather, perpetuating it. This is an invalid cover-up in which neither justice, nor society, nor the person is served. Sometimes it goes by the name of expediency, or "As long as it works, it's OK." But the thorn remains in the body of the enterprise where eventually the wound festers.

When Silence Heals

Love does not wink at injustice, neither does it broadcast the error. Does this mean a cover-up of silence? No. Love will speak the truth in love to the person involved and call upon him to repent. If public restitution or confession is required, then love will stand by to give the person the courage to do so. Love and justice must always walk hand in hand. God still runs a moral shop and will not countenance untruth or injustice. But, bless Him, He is also a forgiving and gracious God who cleanses and redeems; that is the ultimate purpose of His love. When someone is working out sin in a group, we cover him with silence and confidentiality until he is ready to take the proper public action, if such is needed.

Criteria for Confidentiality

There is a practical reason for confidentiality in close relationships. When we love someone, one of our major goals is to bring that person to the highest level of maturity as quickly as possible. We want to help him remove the debris from his life, not create more of it. We want to encourage him to strengthen his relationships, not disrupt them—perhaps beyond the possibility of reconciliation. We want to give him reason to trust, so that instead of using his energy in self-defense, he can use it to grow. And only when he can trust others can he become aware of the resources for his life.

Why Talk?

A teacher who asked a new colleague to have lunch with her became uncomfortable when the other woman began to talk about her son. "We really didn't know each other at all," she said, "and we weren't sitting there five minutes before she began telling me the most personal details about the boy's life. Honestly, I resented it on behalf of the boy!"

Was the mother right to tell so much to a relative stranger? True, some people evoke a great deal of confidence quickly because they are trustworthy persons and that shines through, even in a new relationship. But in this case the teacher felt her colleague was venting her hostility toward her son and would do the same with anyone who would lend her an ear. That could scarcely be called healing love.

There are three reasons why we might want to share confidential information with someone outside a covenant relationship: (1) if the other person is able to help the covenant partner, (2) if the other person might be hurt by not knowing the facts, and (3) only if the other person can handle the information and can be trusted to respect its confidentiality.

Some years ago I knew a man who, as a counselor, extracted a great deal of personal information from people who came to him in confidence. Gradually these people became aware that the information was no longer private, and the leaks were causing them considerable embarrassment. The counselor had meant no harm; he simply couldn't help telling what he knew. Confidences were like so many stocks and bonds in the portfolio of his ego, and he had to flash them around. Soon his counseling load dwindled; he jealously vied with his colleagues for clients. Things became so tense that their partnership ended. He couldn't understand why until his covenant group finally had to be honest with him.

The Importance of Trust

Just as affirmation forms the basis for a committed relationship, confidentiality provides the atmosphere in which all the other covenant characteristics can function. Without·it, relationships cannot develop, and if the confidence is betrayed, the relationship deteriorates.

My wife has been a part of several covenant groups in the past ten years, and in most, the members contracted to be together for a year or, in some cases, two. In one of the groups, some of the members were public figures, and I expected such people to be reticent about sharing the depths of their lives with each other. But this was one of the most meaningful groups we had ever seen. I didn't know this from being on the inside, because I was not a member of the group. Sometimes Colleen would say, "We had a great meeting today!" but nothing more.

As a minister I knew about some of the crises that had occurred in the lives of some of these people. As someone outside their group, I could see that wounds had been healed, burdens had been lifted, and crises had been lived through. I didn't know the details, but I could see the results. Because these men and women knew that whatever they said in the presence of the group would go no farther, they were able to open their lives to the love of God and the love of others. They had the right to put their lives in order and to choose whom they wanted to help them.

One way to shut down a group quickly is to break the covenant of confidentiality. If someone breaks that confidence, then in all love and honesty he or she must be encountered. In doing so, it may become apparent why this person needs to share such information outside the group, and that in itself can be therapeutic. Until the leak is stopped, the group will have little sense of freedom. The others in covenant will find tough going with their foundering little ship of covenant relationships because of the weight of mistrust that seeped into the process through such a leak.

The covenant of confidentiality is just another way of saying that love covers a multitude of sins. It is a crucial matrix for a successful group.

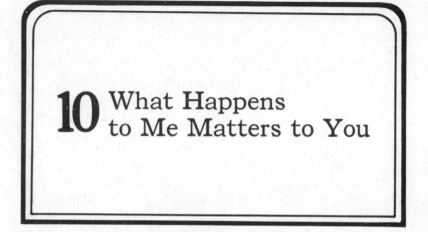

10 What Happens to Me Matters to You

The covenant of accountability: I consider that the gifts God has given me for the common good should be liberated for your benefit. If I should discover areas of my life that are under bondage, hung up, or truncated by my own misdoings or by the scars inflicted by others, I will seek Christ's liberating power through His Holy Spirit and through my covenant partners so that I might give to you more of myself. I am accountable to you to become what God has designed me to be in His loving creation.

My Father, if it be possible, let this cup pass from Me; nevertheless, not as I will, but as Thou wilt (Matthew 26:39).

No one wants to die—that is, no one in his right mind; even Jesus Christ did not want to die. Even though He knew that His death was the will of His Father for the redemption of the world, He didn't leap to the Crucifixion. He told His disciples, with a heavy heart, "My soul is very sorrowful, even to death; remain here, and watch with Me" (Matthew 26:38). The pain of impending death filled His whole being with a deep desire for companionship; He did not want to be alone, though He knew the cross was to be a lonely experience. "Come watch with Me"— or to paraphrase, "Stay awake with Me, don't go to sleep on Me, because I need you"—was a cry coming from the depths of a real man. Jesus did not want to die.

And yet, something of greater motivation came through: "Nevertheless not My will, but Thine, be done" (Luke 22:42). *Accountability!* It ruled the life of our Lord! He considered nothing more important than the will of His Father. He had been sent by the Father (and how many times He reminds us of that), and He was to do the will of the One who sent Him. That was the long and the short of it. He was accountable to God, and He did not count that accountability as detrimental to His personality or His freedom. He was free to carry out His Father's will.

Following the example of his Lord, the Apostle Paul considered himself a debtor to all men, accountable to the nations that knew nothing of Christ. And to those who believed, he felt he was a servant for their benefit. "I am hard pressed between the two. My desire is to depart and be with Christ, for that is far better. But to remain in the flesh is more necessary on your account. Convinced of this, I know that I shall remain and continue with you all, for your progress and joy in the faith" (Philippians 1:23-25).

The theme is simple and powerful: What happens to me matters to you, and I hold myself accountable to my brothers and sisters in the covenant of Christ. To deny this fact is to step out into the desert of isolation and loneliness.

"I'm not hurting anybody but myself," Barb exclaimed emphatically, waving her arm and spilling some of the drink she held shakily in her hand. "Nobody cares what happens to me, anyway."

She was wrong on both counts.

Barb was an alcoholic, though she wouldn't admit it. She was withdrawn from life, sitting at home day after day, never going out even to buy food. She began her day in remorse for the day before; yet she would repeat the procedure: a drink to forget what happened, another to make herself believe that today would be different, and then another and another to dull the pain when she realized it would be the same. By the time her husband came home for dinner, the meal, if it had been started, would be burned and the cook incoherent. No children came home anymore. A son and daughter had left at an early age. Friends had been driven away by angry words over imagined slights.

Yet this woman, who believed that she was hurting no one but herself, had a husband who needed her. He wanted to share his feelings with her. When she was sober, she had a good mind, and he wished he could get more of her feedback on some of the important issues in their lives.

The community had need of Barb's brilliant mind and capable administration, but these were drowned in a river of narcosis. Both her husband and the community needed her and missed her personality and her talents.

Nobody cared what happened to her! That was a lie. Her husband and children felt a pain greater than hers, for there was no drug to dull it. Her deterioration was an agony for them to watch; the children left home because they couldn't stand to look at it. Now they write to her fairly often, and she cries over their letters, but she will not answer them. When they call, the conversation ends in a stream of alcoholic abuse. If they visit, there are angry words and hasty departures.

Barb's mistake was one that many others make; she thought she was accountable to no one. On numerous occasions women in one of the covenant groups tried in vain to get her to know of their love and to get to know her. Time and again both her heart and her door were closed to their efforts. I often wondered what could have happened had she opened herself to a covenant relationship. She did not give the healing love of Christ a chance to touch her.

Love's Accountability

"In the beginning ... God created man in His own image ... male and female He created them. And God blessed them, and God said to them, 'Be fruitful and multiply, and fill the earth and subdue it'" (Genesis 1:1, 27-28). With that great act of trust, God handed His world over to a fledgling race—mankind. For a long while it appeared as though He had made a terrible mistake: Our forebearers proudly spread their peacock tails and strutted about, saying, "We are like God. And after all, who's God accountable to? Nobody! Therefore, we'll make our own rules and dominate anyone we can, because we are like God."

In that distortion of identity, mankind descended into a downward spiral of human emotions that was to build up such speed that at times humanity seemed ready to tear itself to pieces. People existed for the convenience and comfort of the domineering.

Then Jesus Christ came and set us free from our bondage to this sort of decadence. Paul says, "For by grace you have been saved through faith; and this is not your own doing, it is the gift of God. . . . For we are His workmanship, created in Christ Jesus for good works, which God prepared beforehand, that we should walk in them" (Ephesians 2:8, 10).

The writer to the Hebrews declares, "How much more shall the blood of Christ . . . purify your conscience from dead works to serve the living God (Hebrews 9:14).

Freed—thank God, yes! But freed to serve, to walk in God's good works that He had in mind all the time. One word spells it out for us: *accountability.* We are accountable to God from creation through re-creation in Jesus Christ. And if we ever forget it, then life becomes a fetid jungle of opportunism, and the cries of human suffering fill the night. Jesus is Lord, and we are His servants—accountable every moment of our lives.

Accountable to One Another

But we are also accountable to one another. Born into the body of Jesus Christ by the miracle of new birth, we become new creations. The old has indeed passed away, and all things are in the process of becoming new (2 Corinthians 5:17).

Part of the newness and excitement in Christ is the gifts that the Holy Spirit gives us to serve the body. These gifts are given for the common good, that is, for the service of Christ's body and that body's ministry to the world. The gifts we speak of here are the roles or functions that each of us possesses by the will of the Spirit. To be so gifted does not mean that we are superior in such functions, but that we simply have an identity according to our gift, whether it be teaching, preaching, helping others, healing, evangelizing, ministering in prison, creative administrating, or discerning the emotions of another.

The Apostle Paul describes the church of Christ as a body. The body is made up of many members. Each member has his or her functions, which have been determined by the Spirit. When each part is working properly, the body becomes strong and is built up in love, able to do the tasks that our Lord has given to believers as a mandate. When each part is working properly, the world is blessed with the strengths of the various roles of the body of Christ (see 1 Corinthians 12).

Each of us is some cell or member of that body. The cells of our body take from the other cells what they need and so are provided with the resources necessary for growth and work. Then each cell gives to the other cells of the body what they need for their growth. Receiving and giving, needing one another, means one thing: *interdependence.* So close and real is this interdependence that if one member suffers, the other members suffer too. If one member is honored, the whole body rejoices.

William Penn, in his engaging treatise, *Some Fruits of Solitude,* says this about friends: "One is not happy without the other, nor can either of them be miserable alone. As if they could change bodies, they take their turns in Pain as well as in Pleasure; relieving one another in their most adverse Conditions."

But what if the functions or the roles of one of the members are truncated or undeveloped? Then the whole body suffers the loss of that function. We are all poorer due to the undeveloped or imprisoned talent of another. That is why our dear alcoholic woman was so wrong when she said, "I'm not hurting anybody but myself." We needed her, but she wasn't there with her much-needed talents.

And yet there is another "what if." What if resources are available for the healing or the liberation of those gifts? What if there is an opportunity for the development of the function that the body needs? If resources and opportunities are available, then, for the sake of the body, we are obliged to appropriate them! We are accountable to the body to make use of the resources.

Imagine a closely knit team on a special mission to rescue some stranded mountaineers. Each member of the rescue party has been chosen for a special talent needed on the mission. But on the trail, one of the members rams a twig into his leg just above the ankle. The usual first aid is administered, but a day later angry redness surrounds the wound; in a few hours a red streak is working its way up the side of the leg. Dangerous infection! This could mean the crippling of the injured party and the possible failure of the mission. But the medic announces that an antibiotic ointment, which he has, is just the ticket for this sort of infection; however, the injured person refuses to use it, saying in some tough-guy tones that he is going to be all right. The infection continues.

The leader of the party hears about the situation and storms into the tent where the crippled hiker lies feverish and sweating. "Look, Mac, we need your expertise," the leader says. "There's little chance this mission is going to be a success without your help. Quit acting as though you didn't have any responsibility and get on with the antibiotics. You are accountable to this mission and to the lives that are depending on you! Now take the medicine and get healed!"

Take the medicine and get healed!

That is what Jesus Christ is telling us. The body of the church and world needs us. If our gifts are bound by past traumas or imprisoned by former tragedies, we are accountable to use the liberating resources Jesus Christ offers. And those resources include the ministries of others. We have no excuse for not using them. Yes, I know the world has taught us to play the tough guy and do it on our own, but the truth is, most of us are languishing in fever and weakness because we will not take the aid God offers us through His people.

The Dynamics of Accountability

How do the dynamics of accountability work in a covenant group? May I suggest four steps that I have seen work in the groups in which I have been privileged to participate?

1. *There is the dynamic of identification of the bondage.* This will not take place until there is an atmosphere of permission— the permission to share the problem if the principal party is aware of it. If he or she fears ridicule or upbraiding, you can be sure there will be no sharing. This takes us back to the covenants or openness and love. The permitting atmosphere of love says, "You can share your pain and your shortcomings; we love you." Thus the principal party can say, "I am hurting."

If, however, the principal party cannot identify the problem, it may be up to the group to give some aid, and here is where the covenant of honesty comes into play. The group mirrors back to the person what it feels is the enslaving power. And yet it must remain for the principal party to determine for himself what is the nature of the problem. Others simply act as catalysts or resources in the process.

One of the gifts which needs close scrutiny is that of prophecy. Prophecy in its true biblical form is a speaking on God's behalf regarding the past, the present, or the future. However, some would define it as foreseeing future events in history or the lives of others and so claim to foretell what will happen in world events or in the lives of others. Rarely, very rarely, is such foretelling valid, but all too often it becomes a tool of manipulation of others. One may be unconscious of manipulating but so subtle and deep is this temptation "to be like God" in others' lives that we can easily fall prey to it. With authority coming back into the picture of religious life, we humans are easily tempted to misuse it, and evangelical Christians are not immune! It is not our place to make people's decisions for them, nor to short-circuit the processes of insight without which one cannot readily discover his or her need for the Spirit's grace. If it is somebody else's diagnosis, it will probably be somebody else's fault if the prescription doesn't work. We are not only prone to manipulation, but to pushing the blame off onto others and not taking responsibility for our own actions. The purpose of the group in the identification of the problem is to stimulate the principal person to come to grips with the problem and accept the responsibility.

2. *There is the recognition of the causes.* We need to see how these enslavements came to be—what caused the prisons to be erected in the first place. How did these things get into his life?

3. *One must identify the alternatives to bring about a solution and choose the one that appears most effective.*

4. *Having chosen the alternative, one must then lay out a format of action,* which should include specific decisions necessary to carry out the format.

Joan, a member of a covenant group, was bemoaning the fact that she was depressed and discouraged. Through the covenant of honesty, it became apparent to her that she was constantly overscheduling herself, taking on too many responsibilities, and after a sort of manic phase, crumbling into a heap of exhaustion and despondency. The problem was identified as overambition.

As the group centered on Joan that day, she felt the love and willingness of her sisters to work with her, and she trudged back through the years to her high school and college days in which she had done very well but had never been able to satisfy her parents who wanted *summa cum laude,* not just *cum laude.* "Why couldn't you have tried just a little harder and gotten your grades up?" All of life from then on was "try harder" because she wanted her cookies at the end of the day.

The group broke up, leaving Joan with an assignment for the next week. She was to tabulate the alternatives that lay before her to bring about a solution. Her response was so characteristic of her pattern: "But I don't know that I'll have time to do that."

A member of the group replied: "If you're too busy to do that, then you're too busy. We hold you accountable to do your homework."

Under the gun, Joan carved out some time in her frenetic schedule and came the next week with her alternatives:

1. I could continue life as usual, hoping that things might work out.

2. I could move to another community, where I would not have so many friends and involvements, and get off to an easier start.

3. I could stay and begin to say no to any more requests and resign from some of the tasks I am currently doing. This might mean risking the ire of my social colleagues.

Joan decided to stay and fight the battle right where she was, realizing she would be no different in another community and that continuing as she was would mean some kind of tragedy.

She had attended a churchwide creative-planning-process seminar the previous spring in which the members of the committee were oriented into critical path charts and PERT (Performance Effectiveness Rating Training). Part of the procedure was to set times for certain elements. The covenant group asked Joan to come in the next week with a schedule, showing times for rest, times with her children, and times for study and meditation in order to get her head and heart together. The next meeting found her prepared with her PERT chart and a datebook in which she had marked out for months ahead those times for herself and for those things important to her.

Then a showdown occurred. Having made some improvement, she relaxed, dropped her guard, and was soon back in the old habit patterns. Former symptoms of overscheduling, fatigue, and irritability rushed back like an incoming tide. The covenant group recognized the clues and challenged her to her previous decisions regarding priorities. At one point she blurted out, "Get off my back!" but the group would not budge. With sensitive love and warm smiles, they held her accountable. She apologized at a later meeting and then said, "I was really miffed when you caught me regressing to the old patterns, but I also knew a deep feeling of gratefulness because you cared for me.

When you held me accountable to my own decisions, I knew you were right, and I loved you for it. It's tough changing habits, but being held accountable is helping me no end. You know, this is really therapeutic!"

It is obvious in her life. Joan is so much more relaxed and able to enjoy her children and her friends. I have never seen her laugh so freely as the last time I saw her; she was absolutely engaging. Though she is doing fewer things, the quality of her endeavors is definitely up.

The purpose of the covenant of accountability is to stimulate a person to grow and to come to grips with the true nature of the problems of life, accepting the resources available for liberation. Moreover, the covenant of accountability encourages the person to stay in the encounter, continue the engagement, and resist quitting when the work is only half done. It helps a partner to work out the plan.

Some might feel that accountability is a denial of their freedom, but the truth of it is, it is exactly the opposite. When we say in covenant, "I am accountable to you for what I can become for your sake," we are stepping into the realm of satisfaction—a becomer becoming what God meant us to be. What a joy to know that we belong, that we are needed, that we are somebody, and to be able to shout, "What happens to me matters to you!"

11 How Do Covenant Groups Work?

How do the eight covenants fit into the group experience, and how do groups work? The practical aspects have to be part of what could otherwise be a theoretical discussion. Since I am still a novice in the study of the covenant-group experience, my observations are offered as data for consideration in a fast-growing and emerging field.

Families and Covenant Groups

The family really is the basic covenant group. Anything that is said about covenant groups should be worked out in the family as well. The family is the basic building block of any society, and its protection and growth is primary. Coming out a poor second or third in American society today, the family needs to take its first-place position again.

Husbands and wives going into covenant groups need to say to themselves, as individuals, "My commitment to my spouse has priority over all other commitments except to the Lord."

But consider a precaution. Though I know of only two or three instances which warrant this warning, I think it bears acknowledging.

Let us look in on a couple, one of whom feels misunderstood

or unheard by the spouse. In their group is a good listener or comrade in philosophy—*of the opposite sex*—and the stage is set for the proverbial triangle!

Finding understanding, agreement, or ease of communication with the "third party," "party one" is infatuated and yields. "Party two" is shaken by the incident, and the matrimonial boat begins rocking wildly.

My sage Grandfather Evans once said, "There is a great similarity between the loves of spiritual and romantic involvement; one should not confuse the two." Occasionally, the confusion does take place, and this can be unpleasant or painful, especially for the "out" spouse.

For this reason, some people oppose groups: "There, you see, that's just why I don't care for such groups! They get people into trouble!" But if we shield ourselves from all things that might expose us to the possibility of temptation, we would not even get out of bed in the morning but would keep the covers pulled up over our heads. And such isolation is a temptation worse than the first.

Rather, I propose getting into the stream of life while at the same time holding a firm rein on the direction of our emotional involvements. Reining them early is important because once a skittish mount is given a bit of free rein, it is hard to bring it back to docile obedience.

Then too if such an involvement does get going, the group itself can be a tremendous help in aiding one or both parties to see their way through what is so often a transient and short-lived infatuation to a place of insight and forgiveness.

How Do Groups Form?

In some cases within churches, a number of persons may sign up for a conference and find their places in a group by random selection. Or they may sign up for a term of adult nurture and be assigned to groups by a pastor or committee. In my limited observation I have seen a higher percentage of these assigned groups fail to get going than those formed spontaneously.

Spontaneous formation may happen in several ways. When I first came to National Presbyterian Church, a man visited me one day, saying he was hungry for Christian nurture. I agreed to spend an hour and a half a week with him in covenant discipline. The next day I had a similar conversation with a second man; he agreed to call the first man to see if we could make a threesome out of it. Because they knew each other, I left it up to them. Three days later they called back and said they had six others!

We met at Fellowship House in Washington, D.C.—a lovely old home dedicated to the quiet ministry among many government persons. The men asked what sort of groups there were, and I ran down a list of study, action, fellowship, covenant, and sharing groups. When I said *covenant* they seemed especially interested, and I explained what I knew and what the cost would be to enter into the covenants: commitment in time, prayers, energy, and so on. They thought that was what they wanted to do. The next week we were to come back and state whether or not we wanted to "buy in."

As we gathered about the lovely breakfast table in a leaded-glass alcove, one after the other stated his decision to enter into covenant. One man stood, took his orange juice glass, held it out to each of us, and stated his covenant. All the others stood spontaneously, and we drank to our new covenant.

In later times, when emergencies arose in the group and the covenants began to be costly, we were reminded of our little ceremony. None of us doubted that we had "bought in"!

In time, when this group came to the maturity where it wanted to reach out to include others, the members struggled with enlarging the group. They quickly perceived that it would be impractical. Then one suggested that we "cell divide" into three groups, inviting others to join, with the former members being the leadership "starter batch" for each new group. It was this cell-division experience that I have come to trust as a natural way for groups to grow in numbers—the leaven principle.

Is Leadership Needed?

Yes, I think leadership is needed but not necessarily of a professional nature. Bruce Larson, in his exciting book *Relational Revolution* (Word Books), states that there is a mystique about non-professional leadership. We must recognize that covenant groups are not therapy groups in a technical sense, though some wonderful emotional and spiritual, yes, even physical healings, do take place. Rather, these are support groups—communities of love—where love and covenant meet and healings take place.

Training resources abound, thank God! Faith at Work, long a leader in this field; Festivals of Hope, traveling to regional areas under the leadership of Bruce Larson, Keith Miller, and Lloyd Ogilvie; Serendipity Workshops, conducted by Lyman Coleman; and Stan Jones, working with the seminaries on behalf of Faith at Work and Laity Lodge in Texas are just some of those resources that have been a great help to me. At times the churches I have served have invited one of these groups in, or I have taken interested persons to one of the conferences from which they returned as a bed of hot coals ready to set others on fire.

How Long Does a Group Stay Together?

Usually a group forms for a specified contract period. At the end of the time the group may shut down. This gives those who feel they cannot continue an opportunity to leave without feelings of guilt. If the members desire, they can renegotiate another term and perhaps bring others in at that time. This may also be the moment for cell division. After a group has been together five to nine months, there often is an eagerness to expand and include others.

I must be honest here. Some strongly disagree with time-limited covenant groups. To them covenants are for life. There is no short-term covenant. I can understand that belief.

Since the first edition of this book, I have noticed in several instances that when a contract group comes to an end, some feel deserted or forgotten. This is a bit of data I hope others might consider and honestly observe.

On the other hand, when persons move away from one another in a highly mobile society, the covenants are difficult to keep active. We need to face the dynamics posed by these circumstances.

I have also noted that there is always a lingering atmosphere of covenant that persists when a group is disbanded, like the fragrance of a fine perfume. There appears to be a permanent deposit remaining even after the termination of a group.

I have no conclusive answer to the question of how long a group should last. I am confident, however, that God will give His church more understanding as we discover afresh the nature of covenant groups.

Where Do Groups Meet?

Groups meet at their own convenience. This is one of the first items on the agenda for a newly formed group. They may choose breakfast or a morning meeting with no breakfast at all, feeling that eating takes too much time. They may meet for lunch, before dinner (which has not worked out too well in the groups I've seen), evenings, or Saturdays. It depends on the constituents. Weekly meetings seem to be the preferred frequency; meeting more often usually is not possible, and longer periods seem to allow the group to cool off too much.

How Does a Group Start Once It Has Formed?

First, a covenant group should understand the nature of covenant and the commitment asked of each. The group may use the eight covenants listed or some other list of agreements. But each member should be conscious of what he or she is signing up for and then make the covenant firmly. Agreements should include regularity, love, and the priority of other commitments.

The opening phases can be conducted in a variety of ways, as taught at the previously named conferences or in the "Serendipity" books by Lyman Coleman. His book *Beginnings* (Word) from that series is helpful.

It becomes quickly apparent that most of us are pretty well conditioned by our culture to keep us from wearing our hearts on our sleeves; we are self-sufficient, believing that big boys don't cry and that we shouldn't bother others with our problems because they have enough of their own. Many of us find it difficult to deal with the expression of emotions and would rather turn to a more academic discussion.

To help people break loose from such bonds, a number of helps or aids have been discovered, such as the Four Quaker Questions: telling the group about the tent poles (key events) that have shaped your life; bending wire or pipe cleaners into shapes that are symbolic of the dominant elements in your life, and then sharing the symbolism with your group; drawing a picture of your favorite house and your favorite room; or giving a spiritual history of your life in steppingstones of experience. The purpose of these aids is to help you talk about yourself in personal or intimate ways, rather than in statistics or cold facts.

At that point someone who has been through it all before will be very helpful, almost necessary. You will be amazed at how exciting these opening exercises can be and how much people are willing to share themselves when the atmosphere is one of trust and love.

Phases of Group Life

Usually groups start out like gangbusters, excited about the fun as well as the depth of sharing. Laughter and tears mix as new relationships of trust develop, and liberation begins to open up hearts that have been closed for years.

But then, often, there is a sudden silence, and it is deafening! Participants become nervous and disturbed, sometimes guilt-ridden, thinking they have failed or run out of material. It is simply a phenomenon that happens to many groups. We are so under the tyranny of the dramatic that we expect mind-blowing experiences at each meeting, or we think it is all over.

But it is not all over. The group that continues in a discipline of regularity, exercising sensitivity toward one another, is a group that will soon see a regular flow of sharing. Deeper levels of life cannot be shared without a level of confidence being established, and that takes time. Often the silence is evidence of someone struggling with the decision of whether or not to bring out some old long-hidden suitcases filled with highly volatile emotions or some treasured joys that he would very much like to share. He will be watching for the group's continued commitment to the process.

There are plateaus in any living organism. Fast bursts are followed by quiescent periods. Rings on trees, for example, give evidence of periods of fast growth and toughening. So it is with group life. Don't despair. Keep the covenants!

The Place of Bible Study

Bible study has powerful potential for groups but can also be a detriment. If it is handled in an academic, analytical, and impersonal fashion, it can act as a screen to the relational dynamics and shut them down.

If, however, the Bible study relates to life, it can be one of the most exciting forms of Scripture study. In his book *Encounters* from the "Serendipity" series, Lyman Coleman has done a great service to the family of God by helping them insert themselves into the Bible stories and become a part of their reenactment.

Donna had been with a group made up of couples engaged in a relational Bible study. On this particular evening they had been studying the Good Samaritan story (Luke 10). When the meeting was over, Donna was obviously agitated and restless. Someone in our group, sensing this said, "Donna, it's not over for you, is it?"

"No!" she said emphatically. "I don't know what it is, but I need to go over it again."

The group agreed that next week would be Donna's week.

We assembled and were seated in a circle before a fire that had burned down to a bed of glowing coals. The night was chilly; most members wore heavy sweaters and were content to sit close by the fire.

As we read the story again and identified ourselves with the various characters, Donna chose to be the man beaten by the thieves. As she read, her voice choked with emotion as she described those who had passed him by. She had to wait a few moments to get control; it was obvious she was getting close to some buried memories of powerful proportions. Then she began to tell her story in a voice so low it was difficult to hear. I had the feeling she dared not let the feelings out too fast, or they would become an uncontrollable torrent. Anger and pain were mingled with her tears. She told a story of mistreatment by an emotionally disturbed husband and the refusal of her family or minister to help in annulling a short but already tragic marriage. She had been robbed of joy and beaten by a community's insensitivity because of its religious narrowness. But a beautiful man who now sat across the circle from her—her new husband and friend—had helped her regain a sense of worth after the annulment finally had been achieved. Gratitude and tenderness filled her eyes as she looked at the one who had taken her to the inn and dressed her wounds. She had been healed by his love, though the memories still burned.

We had been talking about "trading stamps" mentioned in Eric Berne's book *What Do You Say after You Say Hello?* (Bantam) Trading stamps are those memories of dastardly deeds done by others, carefully glued into our memory book of hate. Every once in a while we cash them in with a flare of hatred or revenge. One of the members asked Donna if she had any books of stamps she wanted to cash in.

"Oh, yes," she spat out. "Three of them!"

"What are you going to do with them? Do you want to cash them in tonight?" Colleen asked.

Donna's eyes turned toward the fire for a moment; she seemed to be staring deep into its luminous center. I was transfixed by her expressions. A look of anger was slowly changing; it was as though a new thought had come to her. Then I thought I saw a smile, ever so slight, curl the corner of her mouth. I had expected a sneer of revenge, but instead it was a soft smile.

She had come to some decision. Suddenly she turned, asked the man next to her for his pencil and paper, and then said, "I'm writing out all my trading stamps. Just give me some time!"

For minutes she wrote without hesitation; the memories were right on top. When she finished, she read over the list. All the pain and mistreatment were there; each stamp was identified.

"If Jesus has forgiven me, then I can't keep these."

With that she went to the fire, threw in the sheets, and watched them burn. Then she turned, crawled like a child to her husband, and put her face in his lap and wept. "They're gone, they're gone!"

"Yes, Donna, they're gone," he said with quiet certainty and finality.

Donna knew the story of the Good Samaritan—by heart! She had related herself to its age-old story and found it was hers.

The Place of Retreats

There are times when a group needs to get away from the pressures of demanding schedules and give itself to protracted periods of prayer and relationship, sometimes for special purposes. On such retreats I have found that recreation has an enlivening effect. Old and young alike get a kick out of volleyball, and those still able to hobble around under the basketball hoops, or toss a football for a big six, return to the meeting room alive with the joy of competition, their blood aerated and their sense of companionship high. Trust seems to flow more easily, and a feeling of knowing one another, which is the basis of so much sharing, is warmly enhanced; male and female barriers are brought lower and age gaps are closed up.

After good meetings, in which a good bit of personal data has been placed on the table and enough discussion has gone back and forth to give the participants food for thought and decision, periods of disciplined silence are like fresh water in a desert expanse. Then to come back and share what God has given in the silence can be a clinching affirmation of the decision made in isolation.

The Place of Pastors

What do you do with pastors in covenant groups?

Include them, I hope. Remember, we pastors are human beings, and that means a couple of things. First, like anyone else, we need affirming and trusting relationships. However, some of us have been trained that a pastor should have no close or intimate relationships in the congregation, as those would cause parishioners to lose respect.

As long as we pastors perpetuate the image that we are somehow above all human struggle or failure, we place ourselves on an unreal pedestal or allow others to put and keep us there. The sooner our parishioners can recognize that we too are sinners saved by the grace of Jesus and growing in His grace through the same processes as they, the sooner will they be able to accept our messages as valid and real, speaking to them on a level of reality they are not prone to doubt. So many folks do not believe that pastors know what is going on in the hard cold world of reality, or that they have the same struggles and temptations. In reality, we are as other men and women; the grace of God works in us as in other people. That truth can validate our message.

A pastor can be a lonely person, often frightened by the immensity of the task before him, whistling in the dark and shouting all the louder because he is not sure of his position. If he can find a group of people who loves him and know that such a group affirms and supports him as a person—being joyful for the pastor's presence, taking delight in him as a person—then often the pastor can open up and find that the congregation becomes to him a blessed family. Let me tell you, as one who has experienced this, I am the richest man in the world! I have not only my family of Colleen, Dan, Tim, Andy, and Jim, but I have brothers and sisters who share my burdens and give me the benefit of their honesty and counsel. And some of them are right in my congregation.

If, on the other hand, covenant group members have a meaningful experience and go back to the church griping and comparing what they have known at a conference with the rather lean life-related fare they are fed at church, they can isolate the pastor very easily. All they need to do is to charge into the pastor's study individually or as a group and tell the pastor how he has failed and how angry and disappointed they are with the lack of relational leadership. Now *that's* how not to make friends and influence people! The problem: the group members have just made themselves a formidable opponent. Defensiveness will drown any possibility of cooperation; hurt professional pride will take the counteroffensive. Talk about debris! It will take half the church's energy to clean up that mess!

While at La Jolla, I had a group come to me, having shared a great life-related experience stimulated by a nonchurch society in the community. One segment of the group came in all bright-eyed and bushy-tailed in their new freedom to encounter. And did they ever encounter! Guilt and anger were heaped high in every direction.

Now, inside myself, I knew they had a point; I had failed in a number of instances mentioned. But, oh, was I defensive! The pain and scars from that one took a long time to heal. I don't know if I ever did reconcile with some of them.

Another segment of the group came and shared the goodness of the experience, saying they wanted me, as pastor, to know what had happened to them because they looked on me as their shepherd. They thanked me for those parts of my ministry that had laid the foundation for this experience. They left, saying that they loved me and supported the ministry of the church and wanted to be available to me in every way they could. From time to time I would get a phone call during the day, and a voice on the other end would say, "Lou, just wanted you to know that I thanked God for you this morning in my prayers." This group also kept me informed of other experiences they were having in the relational scene.

I'll admit I wanted what they had. If something could produce love and community like this, I wanted in! I'll admit I also felt hesitant because it went against what I had learned about a pastor being strong, keeping the respect of his people through a kind of distance and image maintenance. It took me close to two years to respond. *Two years*! How slow can one be? But that's where I was. The thing that brought me around was their love, their affirmation, their sharing, and their perseverance.

Later, I made the decision to enter such an experience myself, which I told earlier. The catalyst was their patience. Thank you, Bob and Honny, Jane, Mary, Gordie, Uli, and Doug, for your love that made a bridge for your pastor, one you called your friend.

Relation of Groups to Professional Therapy

Regrettably, some psychiatrists and counselors deny the role of God or religious experience in the process of emotional healing. Some Freudian schools of thought believe that religious experience is evidence of mental imbalance and the sooner a person can be rid of religion the faster the healing can be accomplished.

It appears that the swing is away from such thinking, and a growing number of people in therapeutic circles advocate religious experience and morals as building blocks of therapy and mental health. Covenant groups are not therapy groups in the technical sense. However, since healthy relationships of love, honesty, sensitivity, and accountability are important elements in any patient's therapy, it should not surprise us if the supportive role of the covenant group becomes a strong factor in emotional healing. Sooner or later psychotherapy must involve community relationships, and a covenant group can be such a community.

What part should secular therapists have in aiding Christians in overcoming emotional problems? They may be of assistance in identifying problems and their sources. If, however, a patient desires rich spiritual resources and growth in the Christian life but has a therapist who belittles these desires, it's time for a change. A therapist who knows God and who is trained to treat emotional problems is the ideal solution.

What then, is the relationship of a covenant group to a therapist? The covenant group can be a great support for the healing process. Since many of our emotional disturbances are caused by unhealthy relationships, so healthy relationships can enhance emotional healing. These relationships can enable us to work out in a segment of society those insights we gain in professional therapy.

12 A Few Results

"Do covenant groups work? What are some of the results?" a pastor asked me with a touch of skepticism in his voice. In all honesty, I had to tell him—yes and no, good and not so good.

Inclusive Love

I told him what I was seeing at the churches I have served where those dynamics were at work—an infusion of inclusive love. Here I was using a term I got from Reuel Howe's book *Survival Plus* (Seabury). Some groups are cliques—self-centered with a dash of superiority and self-satisfaction; all right, let's say it, *exclusive*! Those on the outside may try to get in but cannot; those on the inside look out and thank God they are not as other people. But the inclusive love of which I am speaking is a love that grows out of the health of the dynamics of honesty and openness and God's affirmation and forgiveness toward sinners who can face their sin. There is not much room for superiority here. Instead, a quality change begins to take place in the participants that does not go unnoticed by their friends, who begin asking, "Jake, what is it with you? Something is happening to you."

In a simple way, Jake, who had recently joined a group on

which he unloaded a trainload of heavy baggage, tells his story. He says he has become free in a number of areas but is still in process. As he shares, friends ask how they can get into such a group. Jake asks the covenant group about taking in new members, but the consensus is that it would be impractical to make the group larger.

What was happening? A natural outgrowth of healthy love: *inclusion.* Even though they had felt, under my suggestion, that the group should not take in new members after a certain phase of sharing had been accomplished, they now came to the time where they had to share "this good stuff," as one man put it. They would have to divide and make some room for Jake's friends and others.

God's love is never exclusive. When Christ chose the Twelve to be with Him, He did not intend to exclude the world. Rather, He was setting in motion a precedent for discipling, that is, concentrating on a group of persons so that they in turn could share the kingdom with others after they had arrived at a level of maturity. But then came the great inclusive mandate: "Go into all the world and preach the Gospel to the whole creation" (Mark 16:15).

Dr. Richard C. Halverson, presently chaplain of the United States Senate, was formerly my teacher while he was a pastor at the First Presbyterian Church of Hollywood during the years I was a collegian. Always an exciting teacher, he had stimulated us to be in the continuous process of introducing others to Christ. Therefore when he said, "God is not interested in adding disciples to His kingdom," we were more than ready to argue with him or call him on his inconsistency. He paused dramatically, which was characteristic of his teaching, and then continued. "God wants multiplication by geometric ratio!" He then explained the difference between the results of addition and geometric multiplication. If mass evangelists and individual Christians were to win 50,000 persons a day to Christ, it would take 231 years, based on the present population. Obviously the task would never be finished, because several new generations would have come and gone and the world population would have doubled. But if one Christian were to win another, train him to win another in a year's time, then the two of them win two more within the next year, then those four win four more within the following year and so on, the task would be accomplished in 32 years—in one generation!

That is the principle. What if one group met for several months, then—driven by inclusive love—became two or three groups, those two or three groups became four or six, and so on, how long would it take? In a score of years the church would be turned right side up with apostolic power! God's inclusive love would be multiplying at a geometric rate! *All nations,* indeed!

Do Groups Always Work?

If they did, we would have Utopia now. But, alas, groups do fail.

They fail as groups. At times, the people chemistry just isn't right. The presence of those with severe emotional problems that require special attention keeps the group from being honest or from moving ahead. At times leadership is lacking; the group simply mucks around, socializing, with no one to help it step into the dynamics of openness and honesty.

They fail as persons. Occasionally, members of the group fail to follow through on personal responsibilities, leaving their fellows stranded and without the aid they desperately need. Business, saturated schedules, and problems of their own, restrain some members from the availability they would honesty like to give. They feel badly about the future and wish they could have the opportunity back, but it is gone.

They fail due to withdrawals. "Divorcism" rules so much of our lives today. If we don't get what we want, off we go in a pout, feeling sorry for ourselves, and we don't know how to come back in honesty and in the covenant of "hanging tough." Instead, raised and suckled by a convenience society, starting with formula bottles propped on impersonal pillows in our crib, we have learned well the quick-exit exercises. In building our relationships, we sometimes include huge doors with panic bars marked "Exit." It is our society's favorite way of handling difficult situations. Let a group fail us, and we are out of our seats and heading for the door.

The Westminster Confession of Faith says, "Synods and councils do err . . ." and so do covenant groups. No, they don't always work. Our human frailties are all too prevalent—even in God's house.

Evangelism

Someone said to me years ago, "Where there is specific knowledge of sin, there is specific knowledge of God's grace."

One of the groups of which I had the privilege of being a part turned out to be an evangelistic experience for five of the nine members. Most of the members of the group had been members of one church or another for a good many years. In fact, some in the group were officers of their churches at that time. As they shared their lives, honest needs for Christ became much more apparent. Letting the needs be seen in their true size for the first time, they realized they also had sizable need for Christ's grace. One at a time, and under highly different circumstances, the men professed their faith in Christ and admitted their need for Him. One night, as a group of us were gathered with our wives in one of the homes, an amazingly frank discussion arose concerning a problem in one of the families. The wife honestly expressed doubt that her husband could change those characteristics that had caused her a great deal of pain. The room became silent with tension. Moments went by. It was his voice that broke the silence: "Honey, I can understand why you say that, but I want you to know that something has happened to me that gives me hope. I have let Christ into my life, and that makes all the difference to me. I am confident it will make all the difference to our relationship."

I was to see that man wrestle honestly with one of the large corporations in our country, and he won. He was able to put it in its proper place in his life; he no longer followed his mistress-corporation around with a gold ring in his nose. He was free in Christ.

A beautiful thing about such evangelism is that it not only stimulates a knowledgeable confession of faith and the need of Christ's power to save, but the person is already launched on a course of solid growth with nurturing resources. I have seen new Christians leap ahead in their faith because of the honesty and the love. "Rather, speaking the truth in love, we are to grow up in every way [spiritually, emotionally, relationally, and physically] into Him who is the head, into Christ" (Ephesians 4:15).

Healings

Some years ago, I met with a young man who was struggling with his sexual identity. His story was a casebook example of one type of homosexual beginning. Adopted at infancy, he said his dreams indicated that there might have been an attempt at abortion. His adopted grandmother had moved into the home, and in an almost unbelievably domineering fashion, had taken over the house. When anything went wrong, she insisted it was never her fault and wanted her son and daughter-in-law to make apologies. This incensed my friend, for he thought it was wrong; yet he too participated in the groveling ceremonies and hated himself for it. The grandmother took over the master bedroom, and his mother and father slept in a trailer they bought and placed out back. His dad was Mr. Milquetoast, and his mother an alcoholic. He hated women and mistrusted men.

After two years in a group, he began to see some change in his patterns. He saw how he misused women in his business and got his sexual gratification from men by abasing himself. But then, for the first time in his life, he became dissatisfied with his actions. The Christian love of those in the covenant group gave him a new base of reaction. Several women in the church who became his friends were, he discovered, *not* the manipulating type. Slowly he emerged to a longing in his heart for a committed relationship with a woman. He said it was basically because of his relationship with his covenant brothers. Healthy love was healing him. The last time I saw him, he said that, though for a while the struggle with regression had waged periodically, it was finished now. He has married and says, "It's beautiful; she's so neat; it's getting better all the time." When I see him his eyes have a quiet radiance about them; serenity exudes from his personality—and it began with his covenant brothers.

The clarification of feelings and goals is a crucial factor in the ministry of covenant groups. Through openness and honesty, accountability and affirmation, one has both the permission and the resources to strike out on new life patterns or styles, breaking old bondages and deepening fresh and liberating patterns. Insofar as the old patterns have been the producers or the products of pathology, healing takes their place.

I met for lunch one day with a man who was incredibly angry. I could hardly believe my ears. His story was one of misunderstanding by schoolteachers and fellow students because of a physical malady. He failed to please an uptight religious father; life was a pool filling up with anger. Never had he had a place where his powerful frame and personality did not make others cower.

One Sunday I met him after church. Something was different. He volunteered the story. He had read Colleen's book *Start Loving: The Miracle of Forgiveness* (Doubleday) and had submitted to the love of Christ. The change was obvious; I could scarcely believe the transformation. I saw a tenderness in him begin to emerge. However, the pool of anger had not been totally drained.

He entered a group of men who were strong enough to fend off his periodic eruptions of anger and encouraged him to work out his frustration and anger in creative ways, dealing with his frustration in its early stages. Progressively, he became like a child in expressing his joy in the therapeutic fellowship of covenant brothers. Yet, he still wrestles with frustration. A short time ago I watched him clench his fists in anger, tighten his jaw, and hiss staccato words through his teeth. Then he looked at his fists. A sheepish grin spread into a smile of admission and confession. He relaxed his jaw, opened his hands, rose and gave a bear hug in the man across the circle who had come to meet him halfway. He was in the place of healing—in the covenant love of Christ.

Ministry

Little Denise had pulled a pot of boiling water off the stove and over her face and chest. Her mother heard her scream and before she could rip off the child's heavy corduroy jumper suit, second- and third-degree burns covered large portions of Denise's shoulders and face. Plastic surgeons felt there was little hope that her mouth would have a normal shape. They said it would probably have a wide circle of scar tissue where the sharp corner of the lips should be. Night after night, members of her mother's covenant group brought food and prayed for the little tyke. I remember one evening I could hardly get to the door for the food placed in front of it. When the door finally opened, Denise's father, who had been quite hostile to the church and had bad-mouthed it throughout the community, leaned against the wall with tears running down his cheeks and said, "Why do you do this? You know I can't repay you." I tried as best I could to explain our covenant of love and availability.

Little Denise was healed with almost no vestigal scar tissue. And her daddy? All I can say is, God help anyone who spoke against the church from then on in his presence!

One night Colleen received a call from one of our dedicated public servants whose wife is a good friend of hers. The man was on business far away. That day he had learned from his family doctor that his wife had undergone a test which indicated a need for further surgical exploration. At 9:30 the next morning he asked Colleen to be with his wife as he called her and gave her the troubling news.

During the Watergate imprisonments I watched a number of the prisoners ministered to indefatigably by their covenant brothers. I am astounded at the spiritual and emotional growth that took place during the months of confinement because of the commitment to ministry.

I watched a covenant group gather round a member whose

daughter had run away from home, counseling, calling, praying, and checking in. You should see the gratitude in this man's face when he sees his group.

As a pastor, I am overwhelmed at times with the demands for ministry. I have neither the time, nor the energy, and at times little expertise in meeting the needs. I thank God for these ministering brothers and sisters who have taken their covenants in good faith and are showing the world what it means to be His disciples.

In a world of convenience relationships, where life is easy come and easy go, human personalities are shattered by the shallowness of it all. Our Lord has said that if we have His kind of love for one another, the whole world will know that we are His disciples because of the quality of that love.

At the Last Supper our Lord took a cup and said, "Drink of it, all of you; for this is My blood of the covenant, which is poured out for many for the forgiveness of sins" (Matthew 26:27-28).

He was fulfilling the great covenant God had made with mankind, that one day out of the seed of Abraham every nation on earth should be blessed. Thank God for that covenant!

And Christ was fulfilling the New Covenant that God has promised through Jeremiah: "And no longer shall each man teach his neighbor and each his brother, saying, 'Know the Lord,' for they shall all know Me, from the least of them to the greatest, says the Lord; for I will forgive their iniquity, and I will remember their sin no more," (31:34). Thank God for *that* covenant! God loves us so much that He is a covenant-making God! He desires all of us to drink of the same cup, to be a covenant-making people.

"By this all men will know that you are My disciples, if you have love for one another" (John 13:35). I know of nothing that the world is more hungry for than covenant love. This is our chance! "The whole creation is on tiptoe to see the wonderful sight of the sons of God coming into their own" (Romans 8:19, PH).

Thank God for His covenant love!